SPPARK UP YOUR Marriage

Practical ways to revive love
flames with your partner

DR. SAMUEL PEGUERO COLÓN

SPARK UP YOUR
Marriage

*Practical ways to revive love
flames with your partner*

1ST. ENGLISH EDITION

BOOK TITLE: SPARK UP YOUR MARRIAGE
1st English Edition

PUBLISHED BY:
Createspace, an Amazon Company

COPYRIGHT 2015:
All rights reserved by the author.
5th. Spanish Edition: 2015

ORIGINAL TITLE OF THIS BOOK:
Ponle Chispa a tu Matrimonio

AUTHOR:
Samuel Peguero Colón
E-mail: dr.speguero@hotmail.com
Facebook: Tesoros Familiares

COVER PHOTO:
Dawin Rodriguez

COVER & LAYOUT:
Fernando Castro
pr.fernandocastro@hotmail.com

ENGLISH TRANSLATION:
Shirley Ortiz-Vargas
sop130@aol.com

PROOFREADER:
Lisa Gónzalez

ISBN-13: 978-1518640155
ISBN-10: 151864015X

TABLE OF CONTEXT

Comments about this book

Preface

Prologue 5th edition

DEDICATION

*T*his book is dedicated to a lady whom, after meeting, managed to mark my life deeply. She is also for me an inspiration. What she is, the blessing she has meant to me and what I am when I'm by her side, shows me that she is a woman, friend and wife with beautiful and extraordinary characteristics. Her name is Wirdis, the love of my life.

COMMENTS ABOUT THIS BOOK

I wholeheartedly recommend reading this book with dedication along with your girlfriend/boyfriend, wife/husband. Without a doubt you will be inspired as I was in my early relationship, years ago, through the power of a good book. Reading saved my home and saved my marriage from failure. May that be your experience when you read "Put Sparks in Your Marriage", written by a great professional who, in a pleasant agile language, will direct and guide you along your marriage journey, until you reach a life full of joy and happiness."

Michael Guerrero, MA
Greater New York Conference

"If you are looking for a book full of practical ideas to strengthen your marriage relationship in the core areas of it, this is the book. Dr. Peguero has produced a readable resource, well documented and immediately applicable."

Ariel Manzueta, M.Div
New York City, Family Life Educator

"In this book, Dr. Samuel Peguero approaches, from a social and biblical perspective, the current problem of gender roles and stereotypes and its implications for a successful marriage relationship, something often overlooked in studies on Marriage."

Ronald Rojas
Doctor in Family Life, Andrews University

"In an age where many marriages are submerged in the icy waters of the difficulties that overwhelmed them, "Spark Up Your Marriage" is a useful tool to make every marriage stay afloat. I know this book and its author from the beginning, I've read it since its first Spanish edition, and I can testify that it has been, and still is, a great blessing to every marriage applying it's wise counsel."

José Nuñez Gil, MA
Director of Family Life Ministry, Dominican Union

"This book is the answer to many needs in the context of marriage and family. Its content allows us to open emotional and spiritual doors that only through this material, with its practical approach and to the point may sensitize the person reading it bringing them into a state where they can create awareness to revitalize their marriage relationship and fellowship with God. Few of the books I've read have identified so clearly both the problem and the solution to the needs of households in the world. If you are looking to identify the problems in your marriage, read this book. If you are looking for solutions to revive the flame of sexual attraction that has been lost with your partner, read this book. Especially if you are a Christian and want others to have a clear concept of God and a healthy relationship that glorifies his name, read this book."

Dr. Juan Caicedo Solis
President, Southern Colombian Union

PREFACE

In an age of family regression and marital conflicts, "Spark up you Marriage" is like a breath of fresh air or an oasis in a parched desert. The author's ability to discuss challenging marital issues and make them practical and comprehensible is admirable and his confidence in addressing sensitive topics is commendable.

Gender role of male female has been the subject of discussion since the dawn of time; various movements have either strengthened or weaken this concept. The author was not afraid to put back these roles in their rightful perspectives with dignity and decorum for both genders. His insightful approach to communication and money management, the number one and two major problems in marital conflicts, makes it easier for his readers to understand. His non-threatening way of articulating ways for better money management within the family is adaptable and encouraging.

There is no question that he sees human sexuality as a gift from God, a gift that should be used in its purest sense to enhance the quality of marital life. Hence he provides practical guidelines for intimacy before, during and after sex as well as when facing challenging marital situations, such as pregnancy and tertiary years.

A good book should not be judged just by its content, for that would be a mere academic exercise, but also by: 1) the experience of the writer, 2) the quality of life lived and 3) the examples set. Dr. Samuel Peguero Colon is one such author who has demonstrated in a splendid way a consistent congruence between content of book and character of author.

"Spark up your marriage" is a spark for families and I gladly recommend this book and endorse its contents.

Dr. Alanzo H. Smith
Ministerial Secretary and Family & Men's ministry Director, GNYC
Licensed Marriage & Family Therapist
Licensed Mental Health Counselor
Psychotherapist

PROLOGUE

*T*here is no doubt that the book you hold in your hands will fill you with practical knowledge in the field of marital relations, which you can use to strengthen your own marriage relationship. At the same time, you can use the knowledge to help others.

"SPARK UP YOUR MARRIAGE" will serve not only as a work of personal reference, but as a tool to guide others. In it, Dr. Samuel Peguero uses simple, practical language, without neglecting the intellectual aspect as a writer skilled in the art, which appeals to experts in the field of marriage counseling, as well as counselors, pastors, etc., and while those whose preparation does not lead them to reach that level, but who are interested in learning to help or personally take advantage or its content.

On the other hand, Dr. Peguero ensures that the contents of the book covers a great "spectrum" in marriage. In other words, when you took the book in your hands suddenly his title led you to believe that the author would focus on one aspect of such a relationship – it could be that you thought of caresses, the sexual aspect or romantic activities in general – however, when you read it you find that the book is compressive and includes virtually every aspect of marital relations to give it strength and of course, put "SPARKS" in it!

There is an interesting mix in the contents of the book between the serious and good humor that makes it a pleasant, smooth and entertaining read. No doubt, dear reader, that you'll enjoy reading it. Finally you find cleary defined in *"SPARK UP YOUR MARRIAGE"* the spiritual aspect, without which no marriage will have sparks, or survive. *Enjoy* reading this book, practice it and share it!

Dr. Dionisio Olivo
Vice-President and Director of Family Ministries, Atlantic Union Conference

CONDITION OF GENDER MALE/ FEMALE: DRAMATIC REALITIES

CHAPTER 1

CHALLENGED TO BE A MAN

*S*ome cultures have taught that gender status plays an important role in the domestic, public and private aspects of life. It is easy to see that from before birth, preparations and preferences may differ depending on the sex of the baby being expected. Consciously or not, the inequalities expressed permeate from there to various types of relationships, including marriage.

Some behaviors seen in a couple's life and that many have come to be accepted as "normal", could be better understood after considering the importance of this topic. Understanding the differences between men and women, the way these have been understood and their respective spiritual focus can help achieve a better approach between two human beings of complementary sexes. Therefore, in order to put the spark back into your marriage and prevent it from becoming extinct, it would be healthy to take a look at what it means to be born male or female and dispassionately evaluate ourselves, in order to continually grow into a healthy marriage relationship.

What is: Male or Female?

Many years ago in a place of this earth, a young couple was looking forward to the arrival of their baby. With wine, laughter and a festive mood celebrating the prompt and desired arrival. Already feeling the pain... cannot wait anymore... She is in hospital in the birthing process. He goes to do some errands...

Affairs of men ... Upon returning, there is the product. But, "What is it: female or male?". "My love, it is a boy." - Mary answered. "That's it! It will be a hairy-chested man! Will be named after his dad!"

All is going well so far, but in many cases the story begins to change, if the biological sex is different than expected. The differences observed between genders mainly focus on the biological, with what the individual is born, internal and especially psychological processes, cultural aspects, which can switch between religions, ideologies and even generations.[1]

Being born boy or girl is something that the newborn never asked for. Beyond these common questions that arise from the sexual differentiation, such as: How will the baby be dressed? What color will we paint the room? What kind of toys will the baby have? We raise other questions that have to do with expectations, roles and criteria of cultural mapping, among others. Many seem to have embraced the idea that having a daughter is good, but having a son is a privilege.

In some places, being born male means better treatment, more freedom and consideration and special privileges. Think of yourself for a moment, whether male or female. What did it represent for you being born male or female, in relation to your siblings and the treatment of your parents toward you? Whether or not it is our desire, culture plays a starring role in how we conceive things as adequate or inadequate, as true or false, and in a way, it imposes a label saying what and how each one should behave.

The "Label" of Culture

Commonly we hear phrases like: "Act like a man", "hit hard, like a man", "eat like a man," "think like a man" and many others. According to what we have learned, there are specific expectations that define a man and that are generally accepted. Every man who wishes to be considered as such must meet these expectations. Hence, many men are told with an air of frustration, "But you do not look like a man ..." or even worse, the statement "No, you're not a man."

In his social, family and work world, a man created by the cultural allocation and the historical continuity of many towns, must be able to respond with the corresponding decorum in each situation. He is not fooled by anyone and will take advantage of everything. If a guy is going to become a man and has a desire to cry for some reason, immediately he receives a rebuke from his parents or an adult, who tells him: "Dry those tears. Men do not cry." In other words, to be considered a "man" he must learn to suppress his feelings and hide his emotions.

If someone hits him, he too must inevitably hit, nor can it be left like that, even if he is not physically able to compete with the opponent; otherwise, the parent might say, "My son, do not let anyone hit you. If you let anyone hit you, when you get home, I will beat you again. "The child is in a dilemma:" I cannot fight with that person who is much bigger than me, but if I don't try to be a little more aggressive, surely my dad will beat me up."

Each person constructs their own identity, starting with a positive relationship seeking to identify with it, and a negative relationship, wanting to be different from it. From there that man is forming his ideal of self-sufficiency from a sense of mastery of their environment.

Bonino Méndez highlights that hegemonic masculinity is built on four main pillars:

1. _**Not having anything feminine**_. The absolute dis-identification of any feminine trait is vital for someone to be considered truly man. For instance: Passivity, externalize

emotions, tasks assigned to women, among others, must be absolutely out of their characteristics. This has penetrated so deeply that in a house where several women, sometimes it is not allowed for the man to wash dishes, clean the bathroom and so on. If as an adult a man notices that his friend helps his wife with household chores, or if he notices that he is somewhat peaceful and expressive, the first tries to "educate" the second, so he does not lose his identity as a man and will not damage their group.

2. ***Being an important person.*** Being male is held in the power and potency, and is measured by success, superiority over others, competitiveness, socioeconomic status, ability to be a provider, ownership of reason and admiration that is achieved from others. The fear of man in terms of this pillar is to want to avoid being despised, dominated or feeling failed, so he will make every possible effort to live up to what is expected of him, even when at a significant cost for him.

3. ***Be a hard man.*** This pillar emphasizes that true manhood is displayed when the male is aggressive and bold. Demonstrations involving strength, toughness, ability to assume or face any risk, do anything you want, as long as it solves a problem. If you have to fight, fight; if you have to push, push. The concern here is to be regarded as 'weak', shy or cowardly.

4. ***Send everyone to hell***[1]. According to this concept, man must be a little emotional, keep his emotional distance and hardness. He must stay calm and insensitive to endure whatever comes without complaining and show auto sufficiency to keep hidden his true emotions. "Men do not cry", "silent support". This situation of being self - inhibited emotionally exhibits its consequences when speaking of stress in men, high rates of suicide and substance abuse.

In reality, it is not that men do not have feelings, it is simply that he has not learned to express them. He was not educated or prepared for it. For example: if a man is depressed and his wife asks him what is wrong, it's likely he will say: "Nothing is wrong." However, his behavior reflects that he is different. Occasionally he becomes irritable, sometimes quiet, offensive or evasive, like nothing interests him and does not want anyone to tell him anything. If the wife seeks to address him, he often feels persecuted or pressured.

The domination of women is also one of the matrix beliefs of masculinity. From the patriarchal age, man has learned that being male has greater rights, privileges and opportunities, that among other things, women exist to serve them. According to Christian, quoted by the network of masculinity, the most common hegemonic masculinity contemplates that man prefers the company of other men before any feminine company, unless it's to look for sexual pleasure. Sex, aside from providing pleasure, it's a means of expressing dominance and superiority with relation to women and a way to show superiority with relation to other men.

Don Juan and Fool

Don Juan represents the typical picture of a man. He appears "brave, clever, opportunist, intuitive, observant, rebellious and flatterer... Tries to appear more than he is."[2]He appears to be the popular aspiration of a man and whom at the same time, can generate fear amongst mothers with relation to their daughters.

Tries to conquer and to dishonor all women but cares for his sisters and mother. All outsiders "are or should be" easy for him, but his house, they must be respected and preserve their value. On the one hand, mothers tell their daughters: "My daughter, beware of Don Juan" and on the other hand, parents tell their male children: "My rooster is loose, let them tie their chickens..."

In some places, from childhood the idea of becoming a good "Don Juan" is fed when they properly perform an action that requires bravery and they are told: "You are a good... "The boy, breathless from the approval received from those who are authority figures, he takes it as a motivation that reinforces the behavior practiced.

The other end of Don Juan is the Fool. That is, the man who lacks capacity to face the challenges proper of a hard and hot life which characterize the life of the conventional Don Juan. Most women dislike the idea of having a fool as a companion. Here again the great male dilemma: what I fear and what I desire, with the subsequent question: what is the image you want to project? How do I want them to see me?

Collado (2002) emphasizes that such an approach of the so called Don Juan is also known as the "Chulita Quiteño" of Ecuador, being the bohemian and romantic guy "that is proud of that lineage he does not have and that characterized the middle class of Ecuador for a long time." In Argentina is the "Guapo", romantic character who loves to woo and seduce women. He is brave and exploits women by any means, and is especially distinguished by elegance and conquest. In the Dominican Republic we see a similar character called "The Dominican Thug".[3]

The Cost of being a Man

From the pillars of hegemonic masculinity presented above, commonly, a man feels he has the "duty" of trying to behave at the height of what is really expected of his gender if he does not want to be disqualified, which would be a terrible degradation for him. In reality, it is not easy being a man, and to be it fully is not free. There is also another important element. In some cultures, it is a fact that a man has the "duty" to oppress women, appropriate them, their children, their work, make them invisible, and so on. Failure to comply with this, causes "them to be rejected by other men and even by women themselves. The reason is simple, we all look to others to fulfill the gender identity"[4] generally accepted, otherwise risk being classified as a "mama's boy" or half a man. In this sense, homophobia, or the fear of not being perceived as a real man, leads to exaggerate the rules of masculinity, not excluding the sexual exploitation of women.[5]

Can this situation be considered a "privilege" or "special gift" for being born male? How favorable is this style of education for the current social welfare of families and future generations?

The Man of Value, According to God

Society has taken charge of defining what it sees as "a man of value." However, this concept does not necessarily go hand in hand with God's concept. The Holy Bible says in Genesis 1: 26-27: "And God said, Let us make man in our image, after our likeness: and let them have dominion over the fish of the sea, and over the fowl of the air, and over the cattle, and over all the earth, and over every creeping thing that creepeth upon the earth. So God created man in his own image, in the image of God created he him; male and female created he them."

This passage is making a clear distinction between male and female. To better understand what this means, we need to consider some important details that are extracted from verse 26. After being created, Adam was called to "dominate" over creation, which excluded women. Later, verse 28, says: "And God blessed them, and God said unto them, be fruitful, and multiply, and replenish the earth, and subdue it: and have dominion over the fish of the sea, and over the fowl of the air, and over every living thing that moveth upon the earth."

When looking at the content of this verse we find a description of what this difference does not mean. In his book "The Flame of Yahweh" Dr. Richardson of Andrews University, explains that this difference does not refer to levels, as saying be higher or lower than... nor does it have to do with functions where the contrast between leadership and submission is observed. This difference, then, is of biological and non-hierarchical nature. It should be noted that Adam and Eve were both blessed. Both received from God the responsibility to share their reproductive role.[6] Also, the two were appointed as administrators of the works that God had created. In other words, the two were commissioned to "have dominion" and "subdue" the earth".

On the other hand, in Scriptures we also find a passage that explains the role of women with regards to her husband. Ephesians 5: 22-23 shows that "Wives, submit yourselves unto your own husbands, as unto the Lord. For the husband is the head of the wife, even as Christ is the head of the church, and he is the savior of the body."

The terms "submit yourselves unto your own husbands" and "man is head of the wife" seem to have spread beyond the meaning of its own context. In verse 21, the apostle begins his approach, saying: "Submit to one another out of reverence for God." In other words, the enrichment of the marital relationship happens when a mutual submission in marital interaction occurs.

The comparison used is no particular earthly system, rather cites the relationship Christ has with His church. As head, the model for the husband is Christ. But what kind of head is Christ? He is a head who "loves, serves, unifies, nourishes and shares. The idea is not an authoritarian attitude in which power is abused. Headship implies honor and responsibility".[7] It beckons to question: How has women behaved, being the church, so that Christ, as husband, treats her with such kindness? Still, in his capacity as head, we see Christ who sacrifices himself for the woman. His love for her is indeed stronger than death, to the point that he gives his life for her.

The Bible further advices: "So husbands ought to love their wives as their own bodies. He who loves his wife, loves himself."[8] There is no doubt that these passages present a new concept of what a man of value is. The leadership for which man is called is not coercive. Rather, it is wise, balanced, selfless and loving. He values his wife and considers her a companion, "helper suitable for him."[9] He identifies with "her pain, her complaints, her struggles, her weaknesses, her anxieties and her tensions."[10] With this style, female submission to her husband is not automatic, nor a menial or degrading act, but a duty exercised with inalienable use of their own accord, in a climate of respect and harmony.

In reality, we are all part of a culture. Somehow we have been marked by their influence and even unconsciously, men and women proceed accordingly. We defend it, and we might even disagree with any idea or thing that we deem contrary to or different from what our code perceives as good or valid. That is normal, but not necessarily correct. There are elements that due to the negative impact they have over us and others, need to be reviewed in light of better standards of fairness, seeking to be a better partner and promote a functional family.

Man or Male

For Cortés (1988) being male is not the same as being a man. He notes that "being male is a biological accident, while only an adult can be a man..." "Not all adult men are real men. Some never become one."[11]

Being male, indicates Cortés, is not a simple product that carries that name and that is sold to us via TV advertising, characterized by sexual liberties, debauchery and violent spirit. This style of manhood "only reveals its animal nature ... and is a counterfeit of true manhood."[12] In his view, the falsely called macho man is he who is not afraid of anything or anyone. He is willing to face anyone, wherever and for whatever reason.

Citing Escandon, Cortés, ends by saying that "being a man is feeling ashamed to mock a woman, abusing the weak, lying to the naive. To be human is to understand the need to adopt a discipline based on sound principles and abide by its own deliberate will to that discipline. To be human is to understand that life is not something that is given to us already, but it is an opportunity to do something well done."[13]

Meanwhile, in poetic form Flavio Bazzo, being quoted by Briceño, asks; When did man become man? Then he himself replies that this will happen: "When you no longer confuse selfishness with altruism. Brutality with virility. Slavery with love. Servility with kindness...

...A "man" will only be man ... when he conceives children to love and not to acquire security... when he makes money a means and not an end... when he can be himself and when knowledge drives him to trespass the strange masks ... When tears are accepted and sensitivity processed clinically...

...When you can change the alcohol and heroin for a cry of self-acceptance and when the voice is serene rather than shouted, hysterical... When "man" replaces bars for libraries; stadiums for houses of love; casinos for scientific meetings... When lying gives way to the reality of the facts. When walking is free and safe and when quantity loses its throne for quality... Finally, when man understands that everything will pass..."[14]

Man as a Leader-Servant: What She Wants from Him

When we observe the traditional model of modern man, especially as it is projected today in many cultures and comparing the model described above, we can notice a big difference. It is as if it were a new proposal that brings a rethinking of the popular concept of what it is to be a "man". This new model presents him as a leader who is also a servant. It stands not for his ability to command, but to serve and his ability to serve makes his mandate appreciable.

What does a man who is a Servant-Leader do? Why it is that women eagerly seek this kind of man? There are some essential features that distinguish this type of man. The main thing is that this man has Jesus sitting on the throne of his heart. This man realizes that material things cannot solve the most important problems of life. He understood that looking for solutions that can be appreciated by the senses often complicate things further. For that reason, when the household seemed to disintegrate, when the firm land lost its hardness and simply opened before his helpless feet, this man allowed Jesus to rule his existence and occupy the throne of his heart. Then he was able to see Jesus accomplish a much-needed changes that once seemed impossible.

As Leader - Servant, this man is now in a position to exercise his privileged priestly function in the home. He is happy to share with his family valuable treasures found in Jesus. So the family begins to grow in their relationship with God and among its members.

Also, this man remembers to recognize his wife. Her birthday, her wedding anniversary, something special that she did or is doing, the elegant way she arranges her hair, how beautiful the clothes look on her, among other details. These recognitions give her a message: "You are very special to me", which contributes to the affirmation of self-esteem and emotional security.

For him, helping with tasks such as housework is not a demeaning task. Contrary to this, he understands that to help ease the burden of his companion is rather a privilege. Just as he extends his arms to caress her, the same way they extend to support her and he rejoices to see the results.

Knowing that the lady tends to be generous with words, he listens attentively. The simple fact of knowing she can count on her husbands' ear will give her peace, affirming the relationship. As a Servant-Leader, the man intentionally focuses on making his wife feel that she can count on his support. In matters concerning their spiritual, family, intellectual and professional development it may require some cooperation from her husband. The servant-leader knows that giving due support to his wife strengthens her self-esteem and ability of comprehensive development in life.

Another very important aspect that stands out here is the fact that the relationship with his wife has priority before the parent-child relationship. This man has understood that parenthood is temporary, while the marriage relationship is permanent. He knows that ex-children do not exist, nor ex-fathers, or ex-brothers. However, there are many ex-husbands. Therefore, he works with his wife in strengthening their marital dyad and for the education of their children.

When it comes to intimacy, the Servant-Leader prepares his wife so she can experience greater enjoyment. He knows she needs time and quality, so he anticipates preparing the environment so that together they can reach the desired climax.

Finally, this man has a desire to grow old with her. He knows she is a princess, daughter of the King of kings and Lord of lords, hence he uses his day to day cultivating his youth in such a way that when the youthful charms have been left behind and the passing of the years is evident, they find themselves being closer friends and companions than before. Then, when the King of kings' returns for His children, the Leader-Servant can say, "Here I am, with your daughter, and by your grace, we are here today, happy to go to dwell with you forever."

CHAPTER 2

WOMAN: QUEEN OR SLAVE?

We could say that the birth of a girl represents for her parents an experience that, besides being exciting, is highly satisfactory. However, this is not always the reality. Sometimes you can hear phrases with a tone of sadness like: "No, it is not boy, is a girl..." This simple statement is more than an indicative of sex assignment given to a human being. For many, being a woman is receiving a heavy burden for an inheritance, a horrible sentence. Although not exactly the same in all cultures or stages, from very early in life, ladies are taught to be real women. They are taught to make the bed, prepare food, serve dad and siblings, meet visitors, keep everything clean, do everything you are told without asking questions, be submissive and keep herself pretty. In other words, she is being groomed to belong to others.

Motherhood and the attention of others has been the single biggest project of life for many women. Barna (2011) states that 9 out of 10 Americans marry at some point in their life.[15] We add that if the lady takes to long to marry, for some, this behavior is seen as strange. If a wife and takes long to be a mother, automatically this causes concern in others and even within herself. Everyone wants to know what is happening since socially and culturally she is seen as a dual figure, both the maternal and erotic.

From dawn, a woman will create a long "to do list;" prepare breakfast, get the children ready for school, take care of your husband who is going to work, clean the house, wash clothes, prepare food, go to the supermarket, pick up or receive the children back from school, ensuring that they do their assignments and projects, discipline or be a referee in their fights, iron clothes, attend school meetings, answer calls and take care of visitors. In addition, before bedtime leave everything tidy and organized and prepare in advance for the next day... also she "should" always be ready for her husband and suitable for reproduction. With all of this, the woman does not work, considers the husband, unless she does the same work for pay outside the family circle.

At home, she does everything for love and often is happy with it, even if she is managing a double shift and lives a tired life with little or no recognition. When she takes time for herself, invests resources on herself or does something else for her own benefit, she often feels guilty. The training she has received tells her that to feel good about herself she should be engaged in what any "good woman" would do. Not that female performance in the house is irrelevant, but it should not be her exclusivity. That same way her purpose in life can be much more comprehensive.

The public is left for the man, while she is responsible, or is relegated to the domestic and the private: care of children, attends to the husband and so on. Although women have been gradually winning a major gap in terms of gender, it is fitting to say that... In many scenarios, she is not allowed to get involved in family business, "that's what men are for." Before her man is placed in a superior position which is manifested in almost all spheres: political, hierarchical, familial, and social. Usually, a man does not want to be led by a woman. Sometimes, even a woman prefers a man as her superior as opposed to someone of her own gender.

More than a subject, on occasions, a woman is treated as a thing. An object not only for publicity but as a household object, a decorative piece that cannot voice her ideas, which in turn is passive and does not make decisions. She is on the one hand, a symbol of the erotic, on the other, of the maternal. She is considered the property of man, who has the "right" to use her at his convenience. For example: If a man is beating his wife and a third party tries to intervene, the husband tells the third party: "Do not get into this fight, she is my wife." Assuming that he has the right to do with her as he pleases. And since she is "good", she stays quiet.

Facing the impossibility of verbalizing her feelings and not receiving a treatment marked by gender equality, many women passively suffer in terrible silence the burden imposed by their condition, giving birth to very low self-esteem and high rates of female depression.

Is this Something New?

Let us take a quick look at woman in history. Since ancient times, in the era of patriarchy, we see the polarity of the sexes in a dramatic way. Many ancient cultures, as well as today, had a different way to treat women. In Babylon, the law favored men while it was hard on woman. In Egypt, when you established the marriage contract, the woman could not leave the house without her husband's permission, since it was he who ruled her will.

Moreover, the life of the Greek woman was tied to the dependence of a man, be it her father, husband, son or uncle. The husband was the owner and when he died, he could even assign her in his will. She does not have permission to go to the market, so as not to be seen by other men outside of the family. Her importance was only for her procreative faculty.

In Rome, women could not receive higher education or hold public office. If she talked with anyone other than the family, the husband had full authority to punish her. She lived in separate quarters from her husband and was kept as "another thing" of his property. Already in Judaism she was considered unfit to teach or to acquire knowledge. She was engaged in housework and had nothing to do with political or economic activities. She was part of the trilogy: children, women and slaves who could not even give a blessing for the food.[16]

The various views that raged around women indicated that she should be quiet. That she did not have the image of God given to men and that her existence was justified only by procreation. Tertullian understood that "woman was the cause of the death in man", quoted Estrada, while adding commentary from Teodoro Cullman, who said. "The creation of woman is a dreadful catastrophe."[17]

Women's Liberation

This phrase often sounds like: "Manly" women or "butches." In reality, it is not necessarily so. Just over a century ago, arose in England a movement called women's liberation. Those who advocated for the movement intended to involve women as suffrage with the goal to have, like men, the opportunity to choose their leaders. This is a practice that later went to other places like the United States. Women begin to ask and demand freedom, equal opportunity and the fight was achieving significant results.

This positive action that aimed at equality came to displace the ideals that justified their origin at the emergence of radical feminism. In their struggle, they raise their voice in favor of abortion and sexual freedom; also supporting lesbianism and homosexuality. Also motivates the cessation of marriage as a way to end the sacrifice to which women are subjected. In the case of married women, it stimulates indifference behavior towards her husband, in order to achieve his annihilation.

Fortunately, women today have better living conditions, relative to centuries ago. They have a more active participation in the public and their rights have been taken into account in a better way than long ago. There are institutions of education and support for women's benefits. March 8 of every year was consecrated as International Women's Day and every day more women obtain good jobs and better salaries.

Two different things that we should not confuse are: The emancipation, with the known Liberation of women. Emancipation demands the elimination of all barriers that impede the enjoyment of equal opportunities, salaries and benefits in many fields of human activity. This liberation, however, leads women to role confusion, by wrapping themselves more in male roles and neglecting the female ones.

Women in the Bible

The Bible states that in the beginning God made the light, and stated that "it was good" (Genesis 1: 3-4). Then God created the heavens and the air and declared that "it was good" (Genesis 1: 6-10). God also created vegetation and put over the earth a beautiful green carpet. Seeing what he had done he said "it was good" (Genesis 1: 11-13). In the beginning, God made the sun, moon and stars shining in the sky. In considering the outcome, stated that "it was good" (Genesis 1: 14-18). Similarly God created birds and fish, and watching them said that "it was good" (Genesis 1: 20-21). Then God begins to make farm animals and seeing them stated that "it was good" (Genesis 1: 24-25). Then God created man (Genesis 1:26). There, when he created woman, inspired, he went to see all that he had created and concluded by saying "it was very good" (Genesis 1: 27-31).

This story raises at least three important facts:

1.   God strengthened validation of woman even before she was created. She was not brought into existence until Adam was mentally prepared to receive her. Genesis 1:28 says that God saw Adam's need and said, "Is not Good..." This gives us a clear message of how important it is to God that men go into a marriage relationship fully aware of what it implies.

2.   Scripture reveals that Adam faced a reality: He was alone. This was a problem he could not solve on his own. White notes that "even communion with the angels had not been able to satisfy his desire for sympathy and companionship. There was no one of the same nature and form to love and to be loved."[18]

3.   God then creates a response to the situation: The women. Note that the woman was not an answer in itself, but it was God's response to the situation of Adam. This indicates that if directed by God women could exploit a great capacity to solve difficult problems.

Following the entry of sin, God pronounces a curse on the serpent, on man and the woman. To the serpent He said, "Cursed are you above all livestock and all wild animals! You will crawl on your belly and you will eat dust all the days of your life. To "the woman He said," I will make your pains in childbearing very severe; with painful labor you will give birth to children. Your desire will be for your husband..."

He cursed the man saying, "Cursed is the ground because of you; through painful toil you will eat food from it all the days of your life. It will produce thorns and thistles for you, and you will eat the plants of the field. By the sweat of your brow you will eat your food until you return to the ground..."[19]

Some trace the objectification of women, i.e., considering women as a "thing", to this curse given by God. They believe that Adam was punished with the earth he farmed and not exactly with his person, while Eve received the punishment on her own body. The punishment of Adam was production oriented, while for Eve it was reproduction and the conceding of her desires to her husband.

Dr. Dunker (2003) notes that "despite the patriarchy, women in Israel enjoyed better conditions than their contemporaries in other nations."[20] Among the points mentioned we quote: equal rights that assisted women that were alone, either widowed or divorced, or in case of inheritance (Deuteronomy 24: 1-2; Numbers 30: 3-9; 27: 1-11). The Bible mentions some women like Hulda, Mary and Deborah (2 Kings 22: 8, 10:14-20; Exodus 15:20; Judges 4:5) who had a leading role in the affairs of the people. The proverbs presents women as a business lady, home maker, a wise and exemplary woman (Proverbs 31).[20]

In its sacred pages, the Bible gives women, as a creature of God and highlight of his creation, a special place, much higher than that assigned by history and culture. By emphasizing gender equity, Paul expands: "There is neither Jew nor Greek; neither slave nor free; neither male nor female; for you are all one in Jesus Christ."[22]

Women and Her Life Project

Every woman should ask herself: Why am I here on earth? If the analysis shows that her life revolves around a tight circle, which is only for others and only thinking about the present, there is no doubt that she needs to expand her sphere of growth. If a woman is looking along with her husband, to give their children the best education and care for her home properly, that is right, but not enough. What will happen when there are no children to raise or spouse to attend? Is life over? Sadly it is what many women feel at some point in their lives.

Every woman should have a specific, comprehensive and high purpose for their life, a goal and peak to achieve. Sometimes women seek self-fulfillment aside from their spouse or children, but she will find great satisfaction in taking time to cultivate herself, develop her intellect, her spirit. The best results may not be cheap, but the joy that is felt in achieving her dreams cannot be compared to gold or silver.

A New Male and a New Female

The realities that characterize the popular man are certainly creepy and the challenge he faces is crucial. But, on the other hand, women have also managed to assimilate admirably characteristics of hegemonic masculinity, and aside from expecting such behavior from her own husband, of whom she boasts for not being less of a man than others, shapes her son or daughter in harmony with that same pattern, which in turn is so feared. We wonder, How far will we get? Inevitably, we need a new male and a new female. But these will not be the result of chance or spontaneous emergence.

How to achieve equality between both genders? Is it possible to modify or change the known model of hegemonic masculinity, without falling into another equal or greater evil? Certainly, these questions are difficult to answer. However, society, school or church will be as strong as the weakest home. If we want to achieve significant changes in these sectors, we must look first within the bosom of the family, for she is who forms the world.

It is not so easy to understand what John Piper, quoted by Dr. Crabb, that "mature masculinity is expressed, not in demand of service but in the strength to serve and sacrifice for the sake of the woman."[23] On the other hand, White believes that "Eve was created from a rib taken from Adam's side; that fact meant she should not dominate him as the head, nor should she be humiliated and trampled under his feet as an inferior being, but rather had to be at his side as an equal"[24], both looking for that which pertains to their common interests.

I am looking for a Man

What is the kind of man that every woman craves? In his choicest thoughts, Briceño (1999) tries to broadcast in the following poem, the feeling of a lady regarding that sought and longed for man.

"My search is not simple; in my walk I have seen many men but still continue my search, because what I want is a man.

A man so confident that no matter what my fulfillment as a woman is he would never consider me his rival, but to be eternal companions for each other.

A man who knows my mistakes, accepts them and helps me correct them; who can meet my spiritual values and upon them help me build my world.

A man that with every sunrise will offer me an illusion. That will feed our love with gentleness; for whom a flower delivered with a kiss, is worth more than a jewel sent by messenger.

A man with whom I can talk, that never cuts the bridge of communication and to whom I dare say everything I think, without fear of being judged or that he will be offended. And to be capable to tell me everything, including that he does not love me.

A man who always has his arms outstretched for me to take refuge in them when I feel threatened or unsafe. Who knows his strength and my weakness, but that will never take advantage of them.

A man with open eyes to beauty, who is moved by enthusiasm and loves life intensely. For whom every day is a priceless gift to fully enjoy accepting the pain and joy with equal serenity.

A man who knows how to always be stronger than the obstacles, that is not intimidated because of defeat and for whom setbacks are a stimulus and not an adversity.

A man who respects himself, because he will know to respect others. That never resorts to mockery or offense, demeaning gestures which are more demeaning for whom does them than for the recipient.

A man who enjoys giving and knows how to receive. And who enjoys every minute as if it were his last. When I find him I will love him intensely... A woman."[25]

The Power of a Woman

The need for a man with features like those cited above, does not remove the fact that the woman wields a significant influence. She also has her kingdom, and from there exerts some kind of territorial control.

In her role as a wife can be a great blessing helping to edify the life of her husband. The world has known weak-willed men with poverty of character who joined their lives with women of high principles which made a huge difference in them from that day forward. Others, however, sealed their failure by the type of woman they joined.

As a mother, she is the one who shapes the character of the children. She inspires love, so that they are able to make good decisions and can become self-directed. Similarly, large values are transmitted through her, thus strengthening society.

As a religious leader, she is creative, enthusiastic and realistic. She puts heart into what she does, knows how to motivate people to action and God just uses her for great things.

A powerful woman, is not one that has become large because of her wealth or political influence. Nor is whom submits everyone around to her authority. Is whom has understood her position as a woman is sacred, is the one that can cater to her role as mother and wife in the fear of God and that also has a life project.

What He Wants You to Know About Him

Every woman can develop excellent relational skills with the opposite sex. It is, therefore, vital that she understands the differences that exist between men and women, as this will help create a more harmonious and friendly atmosphere.

A man appreciates it when a woman knows that masculinity is a source of satisfaction for him. He is happy with the fact that he is a man and reacts positively if she highlights that. So to express admiration for those masculine qualities that stand out in your husband you are reinforcing something that is important to him.

With few exceptions, he is poor in expressing emotions and limited in communicating ideas. Because of his training, he did not develop skills to make him rich with words. In fact, the man who is very talkative usually causes concern for his wife. Still, she wants him to talk and it is difficult for some ladies to find a point where they feel fully satisfied with the communication precision of her husband.

Once, a lady went to see her marital therapist and said, "Doctor please fix this man. He barely speaks and is also very 'dry'. I cannot live with him this way." The therapist tried to understand what she meant and proceeded to ask some questions and give her some explanations. After some time working with her husband, the woman returns to the therapist and says, "Doctor, this man went too far, fix him again, please."

It is important that you know that he moves oriented towards his job. Even if you do not like what he does, he is not afraid to work hard because he wants to get his family ahead. For some men, rest and food could be considered as a nuisance at any given time. While this is an extreme position, there is no doubt that if you have a working man, the greatest thing you can do is to support him. If he triumphs, you have succeeded with him, the same in his failures, you two will find yours.

On the other hand, your husband loves to see that you stay well groomed. The care in grooming and personal care that was shown when you were dating is necessary to keep up after the wedding. The elegance of dressing, hair care and the details make a woman even more striking for her husband.

As a man, his pacing is fed by what he sees. The wise wife uses that resource well with remarkable results. She knows that her husband's female coworkers are not very shy and some even show more than they should. On her part, the wise woman maintains her prudence in her dressing, but when sharing with her husband is selective in her outfit so his vision is properly fed.

He also wishes that she considers sex as an important revelation of his love. She, meanwhile, understands that sex is a basic need and therefore tries to satisfy her husband in expressive and creative ways. He wishes that the ambience of the room, the type of clothes she wears to go to bed and her own attitude expressed openness and availability. Continuous production of sperm in the male spontaneously generates the need for it to be properly released. So understanding and meeting mutual needs promotes closeness of the parties in the marriage relationship.

Another important factor in understanding male realities is the fact that, although sometimes it may not seem so, men often believe they can do it all. It seems he believes he is the "incredible man". If this is the case, do not insist. But do not stay away either. When he understands his true reality he appreciates to be given a hand. If when seeing the results the woman uses caution in not doing any fanfare, the man will discover that instead of a competitor, he has gained a partner.

Finally, it is vital that you know that although your husband seems hard, coarse and insensitive, he would hardly be capable of showing prolonged resistance to a feminine treatment that is filled with love, sympathy and tenderness. Do your part with patience, perseverance and prayer, knowing that the God who created the heavens and the earth will compensate with remarkable blessings.

Bibliography references of this section:

1.   Méndez, Bonino. Comunicación Personal [Personal Communication]. Madrid, 1997.

2.   Vargas, V. and Fortunato, N. (2004). Antología Sobre Género [Anthology on Gender. Specialty Works on Marital Therapy]. Dominican Republic: Autonomous University of Santo Domingo.

3.   Collado, L. (2002). El Tíguere Dominicano [The Dominican Punk]. Santo Domingo, Dominican Republic: Editora Collado.

4.   Langarde, M. (1990). Los Hombres [Men]. Independent Article.

5.   Román, F.; González, J.; Fernández, E.; Cruz, E.;

Ávila, M. (2003). Masculino Que Ninguno: Una Perspectiva Socio Personal del Género, el Poder y la Violencia [Masculine Who None: A Socio Personal Perspective of Gender, Power and Violence]. Santo Domingo, Dominican Republic: Editora Centenario.

6.   Richard, D. (2007). Flame of Yahweh, Sexuality in the Old Testament. Peabody, MA: Hendrickson Publishers, Inc.

7.   Taylor, G. (1983). La Familia Auténticamente Cristiana [The Authentically Christian Family]. USA: Editorial Spokesperson.

8.   Ephesians 5:28, 10.

9.   Genesis 2: 18.

10.   Getz, G. (1980). La Medida de Una Familia [The Measure of a Family]. Spain: Editorial CLIE.

11.   Cortés, F. (1999). Un Sitio en la Cumbre [A Place on the Top]. Colombia: APIA.

12.   Id.

13.   Idem.

14.   Briceño, A. (1999). Lo Más Selecto Del Pensamiento Universal [The Most Select of Universal Thought]. Peru: Distribuidora Paper Card.

15.   Barna, G. (2011). Futurecast: What Today's Trends Mean for Tomorrow's World. USA: Tyndale House Publishers, Inc.

16.   Estrada, A. and O. (s/f). ¿Reina o Esclava? [Queen or Slave?] Electronic seminars in PowerPoint.

17.   Id.

18. White, E. (1955). Patriarcas y Profetas [Patriarchs and Prophets]. Colombia: APIA.

19. Genesis 3:14-19.

20. Dunker, J. (2003). Iguales y Diferentes [Same and Different], 2nd. Edition. Santo Domingo, Dominican Republic. Editora Buho.

21. Galatians 3:28.

22. Crabb, L. (1993). Hombres y Mujeres Disfrutando la Diferencia [Men and Women Enjoying the Difference]. Miami, USA: Unilit.

23. White, E. (1959). El Hogar Cristiano [The Christian Home]. Colombia: APIA.

24. Briceño, op cit.

THE MARRIAGE COMMUNICATION

CHAPTER 3

SPOUSAL COMMUNICATION

*O*n a distant region, lived a placid king with his team of servants. Among them was his efficient cook. He was witty in the production of fine delicacies that day to day kept satisfied the palate of the palatial office. One day the king was bothered by a chef mistake. *"I will fire you — he told him angrily - but not before testing your last two meals."*

The cook did not know what to do to avoid complicating the already delicate situation. So he tried to listen carefully to the final order of the king. *"I need - said the king – you to prepare for tomorrow the richest food. I'll have special guests and want to entertain them with the best of your food."*

Very early the cook went to the market, sought fresh provisions, chose his products well, and prepared to do his best food. After lunch, the king commended the excellent cook. His curiosity would not let him hide his concern and asked:

–   What was that so tasty that you have prepared today?
–   "Tongue" - said the cook.
–   "Tongue?" - Asked the king,
–   "Yes Sir, tongue" - he replied. The king was quiet.

After a while he said:

–   "Tomorrow will be your last meal and I will have the most obnoxious guests. Let us prepare a meal then according to their condition, the worst you can imagine. If possible, may it be offensive!"- concluded the king.

The cook remain in thought, and then replied:

–   "Your majesty, whatever you say."

So, when morning arrived he returned to the market and sought the most convenient stores to please the royal request. On tasting, the king admired that he brought the same dish as the day before. Tongue! Irritated he called and asked:

–   "Did I not tell you that today I wanted the worst?"
–   "So I did, my Lord." Said the cook.

But the king was moved when he remarked:

–   "Tongue is certainly the most delicious, used correctly it achieves great feats and wonders. But if you want to damage and destroy, can you show something worse than the tongue?"

Not without reason, the sacred text states: "Death and life are in the power of the tongue, those who love it will eat its fruit."[1] Therefore, the Apostle Peter advises: "Whoever would love life and see good days, let him refrain his tongue from evil and his lips from speaking deceit."[2]

Undoubtedly, to keep the spark in a marriage, one of the main pillars is effective communication. Communication is a dynamic process in which we exchange thoughts, feelings and actions, giving something of myself and getting something from the other person, which increasingly complements the relationship by being able to express ourselves in a frank and warm manner.

It is estimated that in order of importance, poor communication is positioned as one of the main factors causing conflicts in a marriage. However, it is understood that the capacity for good communication is not something we are born with, rather it is a process we learn in the course of life and that we still have time to continue refining.

Essential Elements and Forms of Communication

In his Theory of Human Communication, Watzlawick, et al (1989) emphasizes that one of the axioms of communication is the inability to communicate. He states: "Nor can we say that 'communication' only occurs when it is intentional, conscious or effective, this is when a mutual understanding is achieved."[3] But it is worth noting that it is a compromise between the transmitter and the receiver and this will define in practical terms how the relationship will be.

Fundamentally, the communication process is one alone, provided that the conditions exist for this to occur. That is, a transmitter is essential, coding, a receiver, a message and a channel. With all this in the context of our subject, there are two ways we can express our thoughts and feelings, they are the verbal and non-verbal communication.

**Verbal Communication:** In this type of communication, spoken or written word are used as a bridge to exchange information between people. Verbal language is the result of a context in which certain verbal signs give meaning to communication.

Although there has been remarkable progress in robotics and cybernetics, verbal communication in recent times remains an irreplaceable element in the field of good relationships. In the commercial, labor and social areas, still today, whomever has developed the art of communicating with wisdom plays an important role. The same goes for the family. The higher the growth a couple experiences in this line of conduct, the higher the chances of success they will have in their marital relationship.

**Non-verbal Communication:** Also known as the language of gestures. Virginia Satir states: "A person communicates simultaneously through his gestures, facial expression, posture and body movements, tone of voice and even the way they are dressed"[4]

Although this form of communication does not use the voice as the main element, it has an even greater impact, as confirmed by the study of leading researcher Albert Mehrabian. Only a few decades ago he performed a job looking to decompose the effect of a message. According to his findings, 7% of communication is verbal, 38% voice (tone, shades and other characteristics) and 55% signals and gestures. The same researcher says that if the conversation is face to face, the verbal portion has a component of 35%, while non-verbal affects 65%. Hence, the couple may get better results by maintaining consistency between the verbal and the nonverbal.

The Power of Communication

It is difficult to measure the power of communication, regardless of how it happens. The face of a happy and smiling person can result in a terribly dejected one, according to information received, just as a sad heart can be glad if the news is favorable.

I remember a teacher who once presented an interesting love letter, apparently anonymous. This letter was sent to a bride by her fiancé. I invite you to consider it as if you were that expectant girlfriend, eager to hear from her beloved.

A Curious Love Letter

The great love I said I had for you
is in the past, and I see that my contempt for you
increases every day. When we look at each other,
I hate the way you see me.
the only thing I want to do is

look the other way. I never wanted to
marry you. Our last conversation
was very bland and in no way
left me eager to see you again.
You only think about yourself.
If we were married, I know I would find
life would be very difficult by your side and would not have
pleasure in living with you. I have a heart
to give, but this is not a heart
I desire to give you. No one is more
demanding and selfish, and less
able of taking care of me and helping me than you.
Honestly, I want you to understand that
I speak the truth. You would do me a great favor if you
consider this the end. Do not try to
respond to me. Your letters are full of
things that do not please me. You do not have
real interest in me. Goodbye, yes believe me,
I do not have interest in you either. Please do not think
I'm still your love.

What do you think of this letter? If you were the bride, What would you have done after reading it? Well, do not despair... I invite you to read it again. But this time you will do it skipping every other line. In other words, read only the bold lines and you will see how things change when there is love.

Necessary Aspects for Good Communication

In all communication, we find that it can be functional or dysfunctional. When we communicate a message in a functional manner we try to express the idea correctly and clearly. In the dysfunctional way communication becomes nonspecific and we cannot understand what we are told.

Dysfunctional communication in a family seems to be positively related to anxiety. This contributes to the degeneration of psychological and physical health of an individual, and its effects will undoubtedly be felt on the entire family system. Thus, in the broadest sense we affirm that, functional communication is the same as saying harmony.

Similarly, if we truly want to cultivate a style of marital life with healthy communication, we need to consider these three simple ingredients:

- Express the idea.
- Listen to the idea.
- Understand the message.

The idea we express must be communicated as clearly as possible, using a consistent style of content, body and voice. Its purpose must be well targeted and facilitated in the nicest way possible. Certainly, we need to exercise the ability to communicate so that the other person knows what is happening within us. In this sense and when we understand necessity, we should externalize what are the things that we expect from our partner, what is that thing that I think I know and I want him or her know that is going through my mind, what I plan to do, what are the behaviors that fascinate me and which ones make me feel uncomfortable.

The idea expressed needs to be heard with patience, empathy and without interrupting what the other is telling us. It is beneficial to concentrate in listening to the other person. *"Listening and looking requires full attention. We pay a very high price when we do not see and do not hear accurately and then make assumptions as if they were facts."*[5] *"One of the greatest gifts a person can give another is to listen. It can be an act of love and care... if the husband listens to his wife, she will say, I deserve to be heard"*[6] and this constitutes a lifting factor of her personal worth.

We ask, why is it that sometimes it seems like we do not listen? More than just a casual fact, listening is an intentional act. If speaking with our partner our intention is to defend ourselves, we will possibly make it very difficult to hear. The same way, if at the moment we are analyzing a problem, we harbor some prejudice against the person that is speaking or if we selectively listen, our gift of listening may be stunted.

To understand the message, it is really helpful to avoid rushing the interpretation. Usually we are prone to believe we have the idea before it has finished being expressed. Surprisingly, it has often happened that the next part of the dialogue changes its entire meaning.

Seeking to understand first is the view of Covey (1998), The Seven Habits of Highly Effective Families. He highlights that *"the majority of errors with members of our family are not the result of bad intentions. It's just really that we do not understand. We do not see clearly the others' reasoning."* At the same time he adds that *"There is no way to have rich and rewarding family relationships without real understanding."*[7]

Levels of Communication

There are five levels of communication. They range from the simplest to the most complex. Let's consider our family and try to decide what level we are in and where we think we should be.

1.   *Informal level.* This is the simplest level of communication. In it we try simple and trivial things. In this level, it is used by people who are a little distant and unreliable. Examples of this level are:

–   "Hello my love"
–   "Hello"

- "The day is cold today!"
- "It seems so"

2. ***The second level is used to communicate facts and news.*** You comment on what happened and what is expected to happen. Although there is no significant relevance in relation to the previous level, we have had some progress when looking at couples or family members. Consider an example of this level:

- "What about the children?"
- "They are playing at my sisters"
- "The telephone and electricity receipts arrived today."
- "The food is on the table"

3. ***And on the third level we communicate ideas and opinions.*** Here we add to the information the touch of our ideas. "In this level, we make judgments about other people."[8] Example:

- "I think they should not do that"
- "I see Pedro very thin..."
- "What color should we buy the car?"

4. ***"Level four is, sharing our feelings with those we love.*** We can be vulnerable in this kind of communication. Example:

- "I feel a lot of pain, so much I cannot stop my tears."
- "You cannot imagine how much that treatment bothered me. It's like my heart was broken."

5. ***Level five is the most important level of communication between couples and families.*** *It is Franc and Open Communication, point blank, without hesitation*s. There we expose our inner reality as we feel, without fear. Example:

–   "Two weeks ago I lost my job. We have bills to pay, the children will start school and then some. I went to see about a job, but I'm not as prepared to take it. Anyway, I'll see if I can get it because the truth is that the situation is very difficult."

"Sometimes entire days pass by without no real family dialogue" - expresses Chaij referring to the lower levels of communication - *"Everything is usually limited to a greeting, a single word, a brief comment... Countless marriages remain sick due to the lack of communication."*[9] Surely, we cannot ignore the importance of using single or impersonal communication levels, as long as it is with someone unknown to us or of little confidence; not with those closest to us such as our family. The deep and open communication is a challenge for couples who aspire to reach marital maturity. Only those who can communicate frankly are the ones that find it easier to resolve conflicts and enjoy greater satisfaction in marriage. Adam Jackson, quoted by Briceño (2002), says: "When we learn to communicate and share our feelings and experiences openly and honestly, our life changes."[10]

The lower levels of communication regularly express low confidence and facilitates a type of defensive approach in which *"I win and you lose"* or *"you win and I lose."* In the middle level there is some confidence and a little cooperation. The approach or transaction happens in a respectful way. Finally in the fourth and fifth levels of communication we have a picture of high trust and high cooperation. The approach does not attempt to demonstrate superiority, there are no losers. The matter there is *"win - win"* and the communication conditions are created for it. Andrew (1999) notes that we can speak mouth to mouth or mind to mind, but when we talk heart to heart, only then *"the group fulfills its liberating function."*[11]

CHAPTER 4

IN SEARCH OF POSITIVE COMMUNICATION

*B*efore addressing certain techniques that help us develop positive communication we will consider some barriers that often prevent it. We begin with a brief description of them. In a personal way, both husband and wife will try to ensure that these barriers do not dominate their experience. However, once recognized both may draw a convenient plan to move forward in an ever more constructive and edifying dialogue for the relationship.

Barriers that Impede Good Communication

There are different barriers that affect significantly the process of proper communication, preventing or hindering the growth in this art so necessary in our daily life. Among these barriers are:

• *"We have no time."* Today our homes have become more of a hotel or a restaurant than a home. We barely get up and easily feel we are late, and when we return: there is no time. The truth is that everything that is powerfully important to us will find space in our agenda.

Do we have time to eat? Do we have time for work? Do we have time to freshen up? Why is it that for this and for many other things we find time? Simply because for us such things are important. They are vital things we cannot neglect. If these go well, many others will be under control.

- **"I'm too tired."** *Excessive exhaustion is capable of clouding any wish.* But sometimes it would be good to remember the importance of balance.

- **"Telepathy."** Some suppose that he or she should know *"everything I'm thinking."* Many times we intend for the other to know what we never told them. What's more, we judge and condemn them for it.

- **Assume.** Taking things for granted is a very common practice and at the same time disastrous for good communication. It is better to clearly present the point assumed, and not leave it in the dark for lack of foresight.

- **People or objects in the way.** Before we got married we had family and friends who do not cease to be just because we are married. They continue to be our family and friends, but now there is a difference: our partner ranks first in relation to them. We love them. We share certain things with them and they are very important to us, but if we want to preserve the harmony of the home we must remember and remind them, if necessary, what the limits of each are. Sometimes what comes between the couple is the TV or computer. A lady who attended one of our seminars on family communication presented in New York City stood up after hearing this point and said:

  – "I solved that problem."
  – "How nice! And how did you do it?" I immediately asked.
  – "My husband comes from work and does not say anything. He immediately sits in a chair to watch TV. Me? Work and work. When I could not take it anymore, I put a sign on the TV screen saying: TV for sale, complete with husband." We all laughed at her. But we emphasized that this way clearly shows how not to resolve problems.

• **_Fear of Rejection._** The unpleasant experience of rejection is undoubtedly one of the wounds that most hurts the human heart, especially when it comes from someone we love. The fear of being rejected by a partner prevents many from verbalizing their true feelings, causing polarity in the relationship.

• **_Fear of Ridicule._** The fear of ridicule is sometimes a manifestation of low self-esteem, which is strengthened when one spouse demerits or disqualifies their partner in front of others, rather than being an interested supporter in private and in public. Phrases like "You're crazy" or "You never hit one," among others, rather than creating closeness, it causes distance in any relationship.

• **_Using the Commander Style._** Dr. Norman Wright offers an interesting example of this style: _"He wakes up giving orders. His wife feels the desire to give him the military salute. 'Well, we have ten minutes to get into the kitchen. I want... Come on, get up. First go and take a shower. I'll give you eight minutes..."_[12]

• **_Monopolize the conversation._** Egocentrism leads people to want to make dialogue an experience in which only one is active. It is advisable not to constantly talk even if you have much to say, if you want the conversation to be enjoyable and effective.

• **_Anger and Negative Emotions._** Chaij (1988) considers that _"It is clear that the lack of control with words speaks of uncontrolled feelings. When you feel respect for a loved one, and seek to provide them with affection and understanding, you would never yell at them with hurtful words. Instead you would use soft and pleasant words...."_[13] Instead of a shouting site, the house would be a center of love. So do not yell, unless there is a fire.

How to Communicate in a Positive Manner

Have you heard of someone who is unable to tell their partner what they think or feel (no matter if is about something simple or delicate) without their partner getting angry? I think that is part of what is involved in the art of knowing how to argue and that is what positive communication is all about. It is expressing with sentences such as *"I"* instead of *"You"*, unacceptable behaviors, and those behaviors that make us change color. Sentences expressed in the *"You"* type, will always give reasons for a discussion. Why? Because they appeal to reason and logic, such sentences are perfectly debatable. For example, a wife complains that her husband is always late. In a type you sentence she would say. *"You are always late, I'm tired of telling you and you never listen." "You never..." "You ought to..."* Upon any statements like these, how many beautiful reasons wouldn't he seek to justify his behavior? Maybe he justifies himself to such extent that he intends to make her ask him for forgiveness for what he said. Instead of this style of communication, we suggest the type *"I".*

What is the message type *"I"*? Dr. Youngberg, who for many years was a professor at Andrews University, in Michigan, reveals that these messages do not indicate guilt of the individual in relation to inappropriate behavior. Rather they reflect simple descriptions which express the feelings of the person concerned, so they appeal to emotion and not reason. Where is the difference? That reason can be argumentative, instead feelings, are not discussed. For example: Anyone can argue whether something was done or not, but no one can argue or deny if your partner felt pain, so they did not do what was expected.

Type "I" messages have three parts, says Youngberg:

1.   "I feel - hurt, angry, frustrated, anxious.

2.   When - I do not known at what time my husband will arrive or where he is

3.   Because – I am worried about anything that could happen to him."[14]

Many couples have found in messages type *"I"* a very effective way to express what they feel and achieve the desired objectives. The good news is that there is still room for more couples to join the group that prefers to communicate with their spouse in a way that allows them to achieve better results without hurt feelings.

Secrets to Improve Communication

Achieving good communication does not require magic, but the willingness to do your part to make it happen, as each couple prepares their own travel luggage. The following suggestions will help us build a comfortable and secure communication boat with our partners:

1.   ***Take time to be alone with your spouse.*** Frequently dedicate quality time, accumulate merit or dividends in the emotional bank of your partner.

2.   ***Open and mature dialogue.*** Simple communication levels offer no significant contribution to meaningful relationships.

3.   ***Develop a way to talk that will inspire comfort and trust in your partner.*** This is what it means to speak for the other to listen and listen for the other to speak.

4.   ***Use tact to talk.*** Remember that more important than what we say, is how we say it. Tact is a virtue of the wise.

5.   ***Use positive communication.*** If we are to achieve

the hoped progress in the conduct of our consort, this resource is vital and practical. Maybe we are not used to it, but if we continually practice it, time and results will turn it gratifying.

6.   **Listen carefully.** Set aside all other tasks when you talk to your partner. Give the impression that what they are saying is important to you.

7.   **Try to participate together in a project.** Teamwork strengthens relationships and fosters unity. Being married is also having the opportunity to dream, create and have fun.

8.   **Look into the eyes of your spouse while chatting.** This inspires confidence and it strengthens you more each time.

9.   **Take the feelings and needs of your spouse into account.** To meet these needs, and carefully consider such feelings makes us enjoy a more livable family atmosphere.

10.   **Put yourself in the place of the other and give them their importance.** That is empathy. It should be remembered that the other person is also a human being.

11.   **Practice the touch dialogue.** Touch communication has a therapeutic effect on the couple. Try it, and enjoy the results.

12.   **Use friendly phrases. "I love you." "I miss you." "I was thinking of you." "I have a great desire to be by your side."** Phrases like these cost very little yet are more significant than what we estimate.

13.   **Avoid criticism, negative comments,** *irony,*

talking with others about marital intimacy, unless is in search of professional help."

14. **Communication** is nurtured when you *share* with your partner *those things that transcend* having things or *go beyond issues of money*, i.e., addressing topics such as family, health, emotions, values and principles of good living. But above all, God and his beautiful promise to prepare a beautiful mansion for your family in heaven."

15. ***Show the appreciation and satisfaction we feel for what is done in our favor***, as well as to express admiration for our spouse.

While it is true that we are not born with wise integrated communication strategies, it is no less true that we can incorporate it into our daily style of family interaction. Nobody is born a good athlete, coach or artist, but the development of such skills does make you excel in the area of your choice. This also applies to communication. Removing barriers, the use of positive communication and the healthy forming of techniques will add spark to our marriage, instead of fire.

Bibliography references of this section:

1.   Proverbs 18: 21.

2.   1 Peter 3: 10.

3.   Watzlawick, P.; Beanvin, J.; Jackson, D. (1989). *Teoría de la Comunicación Humana (Theory of Human Communication)*. Barcelona, Spain: Editorial Herder.

4.   Satir, V. (1983). *Psicoterapia Familiar Conjunta [Joint Family Psychotherapy]*. Mexico: The Mexican Medical Press.

5.   Satir, V. (1981). *Relaciones Humanas en el Núcleo*

Familiar [Human Relations in the Family Core]. México: Editorial Pax Mexico.

6. Wright, N. (1994). *Claves Para una Mejor Comnicación en el Matrimonio [Keys to Better a Communication in Marriage].* Colombia: Editorial Unilit.

7. Covey, S. (1998). *Los 7 Hábitos de las Familias Altamente Efectivas [The 7 Habits of Highly Effective Families].* México: Grijalbo.

8. Youngberg, J. M. (2000). *La Familia en su Máximo Potencial [Family at Maximum Potential].* Mexico: Universidad de Montemorelos.

9. Chaij, E. (1992). *Vivir con Valor (Living with Valor).* Colombia: APIA.

10. Briceño, P. (2002). *Lo Más Selecto Del Pensamiento Universal [The Most Select of the Universal Thought].* Lima, Peru.

11. Andres. M. (1999). *Matrimonio Adulto. [Adult Marriage].* Santo Domingo: Ediciones MSC.

12. Op cit (Wright) p. 125.

13. Chaij, E. (1988). *A Pesar de Todo... ¡Que Linda es la Vida! [In Spite of Everything... Life is Beautiful!]* Colombia: APIA.

14. Youngberg, J. and M. (s / f). *Seminario de Bienestar Familiar [Family Welfare Seminar].* Paper Materials for Instructor. Michigan.

SECTION 3
THE COUPLE AND FINANCES

CHAPTER 5

HOW TO MANAGE HOME FINANCES

"$\mathcal{I}$ love you my love, nothing else matters" is the cute phrase exchanged by many couples before marriage. The interesting thing is that later they start to notice, with surprise, that to pay the bills it takes more than love. There are many homes that have sunk deep because of their financial difficulties. Dr. Wood believes that "often anxiety over money matters helps to make family life more miserable than anything else."[1]

We see that one or both partners are working around the clock just to reduce their debts and meet their material needs. However, both feel overwhelmed at seeing their debts rise, while their incomes remain stable. Mortgage, insurance, auto, services and a consort who always wants more money.

Sometimes the problem is not whether there is money or not, it is rather the inadequate management given to the resources. Today, in countries like the United States, the issue of finance, i.e. who controls it, regarding decisions, expenses, savings, budgeting, among other things, constitute in order of importance, the main reason of problems and quarrels between couples.

Why Isn't The Money Enough?

For some, "the saying that the money is never enough" has become a daily reality. Does this have to be this way? Let us consider some of the reasons why that powerful influence, money, is not enough.

1. **Not knowing how to rightly identify what are "needs " and "wants."** Not everything that we want do we really need; and quite often unnecessary things are converted into needs, without taking into account other necessities of our family. To help us with this issue Botting suggests we ask ourselves the following questions: "Do I really need this, or just want to have it? If I do not buy it today, will something terrible happen to me? Why didn't I need it three weeks ago? Will I still need it within three weeks?"[2]

2. **Not having a defined plan of expenses.** Whoever does not tell the money where it is going, will have to find out where it went. We cannot trust that one day we will know. This type of adventure ensures economic ruin.

3. **Inability to handle credit.** It seems that not everyone shows the capacity to manage their credit. *"Pencil tip does not kill anyone"* - goes a popular saying. *"While creditors appears everything seems fine, even if there is no one to pay,"* says Norma Asmar.

Certainly there is never a lack of those who offer. If we listen to all of them because *"we pay it with the credit card"* we can reach a situation of financial drowning. "People who are not willing to sacrifice themselves, and do not stop their whims, impulses and desires, will always live in debt slavery..."[3]

4. **Uncontrolled leakage of resources.** By the way, where are your resources leaking? Figure out where most of your capital is going and note which ones can be trimmed. For many people their money is leaking in: Rent or mortgage, personal ornaments and beauty centers, the car (monthly payment, repairs, maintenance and accessories), transportation services, home decorations, telephone, energy electricity, gas and health issues. For others the leak can be in trips or walks as well as the famous

deals or bargains, especially of those things you do not need and therefore have not budgeted to buy. After a serious analysis it would be convenient to ask: In what things our biggest expenses are concentrated? Can I make an adjustment?

5. **Having an awareness that revenues are few and yet remaining inactive when there are alternatives to increase revenue.** Often with a little more effort and better management, there would be an economic condition that could reduce the financial constraints of the home.

Psychological Effects of Wrong Use of Money

As a biblical passage reads: "Whatever a man sows, that he shall also reap."[4] An emotional or inadequate management of household finances will bring significant consequences that will somehow affect the whole family. One way in which the effect is manifested in the serious concerns it causes. A person full of debt will be a concerned person. Financial crises can produce despair, stress, anxiety, lack of appetite, and sleep problems.

Another result of misuse of money that we can considerate is the effect on self-esteem. The continued *"I cannot"* or *"I don't have"* can help accommodate a sense of failure and self - marginalization. For many people their economic capacity is symbolic of their value. Previously they used to say: *"Tell me who your friends are and I will tell you who you are"*, today is more common to inquire: *"Tell me what you have and I will tell you who you are."*

While certainly a human being is much more than money, the economic level remains for many an important factor in the feeling and building of their own self-esteem. Think of the child who could not participate with his classmates at the scheduled activity because he had no money to pay, which has happened before. How did he feel in relation to his peers?

For many people money is a symbol of joy and is also credited with the power to influence sadness. If a person is told that for this or that reason they have been awarded by their employer and have earned a special bonus of $150,000, what do you think will happen to the person? See how the eyes would immediately shine with excitement and joy. But if that same person is informed that the bank where they have kept their life resources just declared bankruptcy, What will happen to that face? Probably changes in their face, their voice becomes hoarse, the person becomes sad and pensive, cries, etc.

When good humor and enthusiastic mood does not depend on the amount of money available, then man will have achieved a great victory. John Wicker said: "Wealth does not consist in making money, but in making the man while he makes the money." (Cited by Botting, op cit p 7)[5]

The uncontrolled or misuse of money is also a powerful way that many spouses use to draw attention to their consorts. For example: Donna is married to Jeffry but feels neglected by him, so she takes the credit card and gives it a disproportionate use looking to get the attention that she longs from her husband. He reacts upset with her, however, she managed to get him out of *"his world"* to place him where she needed him. This is, without a doubt, a strange and wrong way to build camaraderie between partners.

What Kind of Shopper Are You?

Certain individuals retain close affinity with some of the different types of buyers we will see below.

• In the first row, who purchases because they desire something, not because they need it. No matter if they do not need it. Maybe they went to the store get something, but used the money for something else and then thinks about what they really went out to get. Regardless of how much they accumulate, this person tends to feel dissatisfied because "whoever loves wealth is never satisfied with his income. This also is vanity,"[6] revealed the wise Solomon.

• In the second line, are grouped those who buy to collect, who are only interested in increasing their collection. This person is happy collecting things, even if they have to pay money today that tomorrow will be needed. It is also possible that such a person does not have any additional space in their home to store everything else they feel like bringing in. There is an old saying: "Do not buy what you do not need, because then you will have to sell what you need most, to pay for what you do not need."

• And finally there are those that buy for competition. These, in turn, are good for observing and imitating. They observe what furniture or car is bought by their neighbor, what new details accompany it, and to keep up, they buy something that is better.[7]

Keys to Making Your Financial Plan Succeed

Continually to lament over the economic crisis will not solve the problem because lamenting does not rectify the problem. Having a defined plan of expenses, however, is vital so a family can achieve financial freedom. Such, accompanied by action, is preferable than the best of wishes. In the field of personal and family finance management there are some tips, that if persistently applied, can make the difference between a successful employee and an employer in endless crisis.

1. *Plan your future.* Every family needs to have their goals. Living just to see what will happen brings no satisfaction. Determine what to do, how and when. The couple who wants to be successful in their finances will take time to draw challenging

but realistic plans, to be realized in a short, medium and on a long term basis. The reason why this issue is so important is that if you do decide to plan your future, then you have already decided that your future will plan you.

Do not lose sight of the goal that has been set. Remember that to accomplish what you want you will need a process that will require firmness and patience, [8] but that can be achieved. Some motivational experts recommend constantly remembering why these goals have been set. They argue that by constant repetition we will always remember why we are making the sacrifice. They note that this will give each new day forces to continue the arduous task that requires achieving the goal that has been set.[9]

2. ***Involve your whole family.*** Although not every family member produces money there are several advantages to everyone being involved. This style gives economic direction to the family, fosters unity of the system, avoids many problems about money and facilitates team collaboration. The member who only knows that there are a lot of expenses can possibly find a way to express their dissatisfaction.

If there are children in the house, it is equally important for them to participate in the preparation of the financial plan. This way they will learn and adopt an attitude of commitment and collaboration.

3. ***Establish with clarity what your priorities are.*** After making a list of things that we understand are necessary, we have to identify which ones should be given preference and which must wait until a later date. Some families have established a habit of meeting before the end of the year, and then after reviewing and evaluating the execution of the years plan, together they define the priorities for the next period.

4. ***Have a family budget.*** This instrument, if done as a

team, will help prevent a host of demands at inopportune times; it will give better guidance to the expenses and provide for certain emergencies. Note that "it is not always fun budgeting, but the only way to follow and apply what you've learned about how to get out of debt, save and share even while satisfying basic needs."[10] When there is no defined plan of expenses there are problems with stretching resources. Later we will expand on this aspect.

5. **Save.** Someone said: "Whoever saves when you have, will eat when you want", but, what if the money is not enough to save? Remember that money, as well as time, is never enough. However, when planning it can be listed as an available value. Think for a moment of all the effort of your hard work, the only thing that is truly yours is what you save. No matter how much you earn if everything goes to pay, how will you face the financial contingencies that arrive without warning, but that throw us off balance? Save, that is, "Pay yourself first" advises Carol Keeffe.[11]

Certainly there are bills to pay, but if you work a week or a month and at the end all the money is for your commitments, who will pay you? How will you cover your expenses when your strength is gone? On the other hand, if you prefer not saving now because your income is small, what will you do when you are unable to work? If, however, you save everything and enjoy little or nothing, if it hurts to set aside some amount for recreation, one day, perhaps consistent with Katherine Keeffe Jonson, who concluded: "Tell them to enjoy it while they can, not like us. When you're in the eighties and have the money, but cannot go."[12] Dedicating to savings even a small percentage is to open a new life in the present and the future for ourselves and for our family.

6. **Close the money leaks.** Everything we spend our resources on is *"important"* for us. But is it really necessary or

is it simply an unnecessary expense? We cannot always have what we want when we want it, but if we decide to have it, let us be sure that such things are part of the solution and not part of the problem.

7. **Giving for the needs of others** is one of the principles recommended by the renowned financial expert Larry Burkett. Question: *"What is a distant relative?"* And he answered: *"It is a close relative to whom you have lend money..."* *"Avoid lending money to a person — he adds - if it is possible to give... the testimony and fellowship that occurs as a result is more permanent than temporary appreciation resulting from a loan and that soon disappears"*[13] Not without reason the sacred text says: *"Blessed are those who have regard for the weak; the Lord delivers them in times of trouble. The Lord protects and preserves them, they are counted among the blessed in the land, and He does not give them over to the desire of their foes."*[14] Whoever is kind to the poor lends to the Lord, and he will reward them for what they have done"[15]

8. **Remember who the owner is.** We bring nothing when we come to this world and can take nothing with us on our final day. However, egotism is still the evil of our time. Who will own the world? David replies: "Earth is the Lord's and the fullness thereof; the world and those who dwell therein. For he hath founded it upon the seas and established it upon the floods."[16]

According to this principle God owns everything, including our own life with everything we have. We are stewards or temporary administrators. On this basis a large number of people have understood and applied the principle of tithing, i.e. dedicate a tenth of their earnings for the religious development of their faith community.

Speaking about financial freedom the renowned financier Burkett encourages: "Decide to give God the first part of your income in recognition that everything belongs to Him... This is an essential step in economic breathing."[17] Reid also considers it this way when he adds that "to succeed as managers we must understand the principle of property of God."[18] In this respect, today you can enjoy positive results.

9. ***Remember this: Invest!*** Allocating your money to savings with the sole purpose of it staying there year after year, is not such a great idea. Good investments ensure a more significant growth of your money and less fear of devaluation.

In the next chapter we will cover a topic that, despite being undesirable, can surprise us at any time: Preventing and facing financial crisis.

CHAPTER 6

PREVENTING AND DEALING
WITH FINANCIAL CRISIS

In a home where there is frugality, the wise administration marches by the hand of the plan that was previously designed and that is executed with discipline. Unfortunately, many good plans of development and financial freedom have remained stagnant by remaining as simple desires that fail to be considered in a budget.

So what is a budget? It is a self-management plan of expenses that helps us organize our payments and to save some money. This plan we impose on ourselves allows us to have money available for things we really need, while helping us avoid those expenses that could or should be avoided. In addition, it motivates family discipline in economic management. Let us remember that in our home life, a consistent model is more powerful than the spoken speech of a lifetime.

A budget shows income, which are the resources that you have and can count on, and expenses. Remember well what your goals are, then place all income received, either weekly, bi-weekly or monthly, including those items that are not fixed, but that can be estimated. Then consider the expenses. These could be: fixed, sporadic or unexpected.

It is recommended to include in the budget a provision for creating the family emergency fund, "ideally, it should be the equivalent of the household income of two quarters." This time would help us recover in the event of facing a common emergency.

Who will manage the budget? Although the budget should be handled with combined resources, if both work, it is advised that one of you should be in charge of managing the accounts, addressing the major expenditures and controlling diverse expenses. A wise partner would assign this to the party demonstrating a better capacity of management and cost control, no matter which one it is. Let us practice a suggestive idea of what would be a family budget:

BUDGET MODEL

INCOME	
His Salary	
Her Salary	
Interest income	
Other income	
TOTAL REVENUE	
Fixed Expenses	
Tithes and Offerings	
Savings	
Food	
Educational Affairs	
Insurance	
Medical expenses	
Housing or rental payment	
Car payment / maintenance	
Debt payments	
Yours	
Mine	
Vacations	
Recreation	
Flexible Spending	
Utility payments	
Household items	
Other expenses	
Unforeseen expenses	
TOTAL EXPENDITURE	

First Aid When there is Financial Crisis

A good starting point to achieve reorganization of personal and family finances is putting aside obstacles often consciously or unconsciously many people self-imposed. They are often pretexts that instead of helping, hinder progress. "It's your fault", "we have little money", "is not enough for us", [19] among others, are blockages that we impose ourselves.

Job loss, a lawsuit, a catastrophic event such as an illness or accident, or simply a wrong decision can lead any individual or family to financial crisis. If such a thing exists, pretending to ignore that reality is sinking deeper into poverty. Difficult situations have to be faced with courage. When financial crisis exists expenditures exceed income and we have no control over the first one. Debts are an endless chain and stressful situations dominate every day. In this situation what can we do? Here are some tips that might be helpful:

1.   Avoid committing to new debts.

2.   Make a plan of family austerity where you remove anything that can be removed. Avoid those privileges that sometimes you engage in. We are facing a crisis and we need the involvement of the entire team.

3.   Pay your bills. List each from highest to lowest. Try to remove the smaller debts first. This will give you a gradual sense of liberation and satisfaction and allow you to have more available to meet your other debts. Sometimes it may be necessary to sell some items to cancel certain debts, as recommended by some of the financiers mentioned above.

4.   Check your credit cards well. In the time in which we live they are a necessary tool, unless they "inhibit" the individual of his/her freedom and self-control.

God does not want his children to have financial crisis, rather, for everyone He wants prosperity. So said John when he said: "Beloved, I pray that you may prosper in all things..."[20] for that reason he left us valuable advice so we could tell a better story. God does not grieve when he sees that His children are enriched with dignity, however His riches are greater than our own. But to spare us the agony of excessive desire to acquire and accumulate assets He reminds us, *"Watch out! Be on your guard against all kinds of greed; life does not consist in an abundance of possessions."21*

Remember that the true value of a human being, of family and life is not measured in euros, dollars or pesos. A human beings' worth is above what you may have. Although money is certainly a very important resource for the security and stability of the family; as well as to assist in having a better lifestyle. It would be good to try to acquire and achieve financial freedom, without being a slave to it, and without it robbing us of peace. This advice is well illustrated by Omar Medina in his valuable *"To Encourage a Heart"* compilation, with his story The 99 Circle. Let us see what this is about:

"There once was a very sad king who had a servant who was very happy. Every morning he came to bring breakfast and wake the king smiling and humming happy songs. A smile on his distended face and his relaxed attitude towards life which was always serene and cheerful. One day the king summoned him.

- Servant – he said - What is the secret?
- What secret, your Highness?
- What is the secret of such joy?
- There is no secret, your Majesty.
- Servant, do not lie. I have ordered some to be beheaded for lesser offenses than a lie.
- I'm not lying, your Highness, I'm not keeping any secrets.
- Why are you always cheerful and happy? Huh? Why?

     –   Majesty, I have no reason to be sad. Your Highness honors me letting me serve you. I have my wife and children living in the house that the Court has assigned to us, we are clothed and fed and also his Highness rewards us occasionally with some coins so we can indulge in something we may want, why not be happy?

     –   If you do not tell me the secret now, I will have you beheaded – said the king - nobody can be happy for those reasons you have given.

     –   But, Your Majesty, there is no secret. I would like nothing more than to please you, but there is nothing that I am hiding...

     –   Leave. Leave before I call the executioner!

The servant smiled, bowed and left the room. The king became crazy. He could not explain how the servant was happy living on borrowed time, using old clothes and feeding on scraps of courtiers. When he calmed down, he called the wisest of his advisers and told him about his morning conversation.

     –   Why is he happy?

     –   Ah, your Majesty, what happens is that he is outside of the circle.

     –   Out of the circle?

     –   That's it.

     –   And that is what makes him happy?

     –   No, your Majesty that is what makes him not unhappy.

     –   Let me see if I understand, being in the circle makes you unhappy.

     –   That's it.

     –   And how did he leave?

     –   He never entered!

     –   Which circle is that?

     –   Circle 99.

—   I really do not understand anything.

—   The only way to understand, would be showing with facts.

—   How?

—   Making the servant enter the circle.

—   That's it, let's force him to enter!

—   No, your Highness, no one can force anyone to enter the circle.

—   Then you have to deceive him.

—   No need, your Majesty. If we give him the opportunity, he will enter the circle all on his own.

—   But will he realize that this is his unhappiness?

—   Then he will not enter.

—   He will not be able to avoid it.

—   You say that he will realize the unhappiness that will be caused by that ridiculous circle, and still enter it and not be able to get out?

—   Yes your Majesty. Are you willing to lose an excellent servant to understand the structure of the circle?

—   OK. Tonight I will stop by to get you. You must prepare a small wooden box with 99 gold coins. No more no less. 99!

—   What else? Should I take the guards just in case?

—   Nothing else but the wooden box with coins. Your Majesty, until tonight.

—   Until tonight.

And so it was. The wise man went to get the king. Together they slipped through the palace courtyards and hid near the house of the servant. When indoors the first candle was lit, the wise man took the box and put a paper saying: *"This treasure is yours. It is the reward for being a good man. Enjoy it and do not tell anyone how you found it."*

Then he tied the paper to the box and put it at the door of

the servant, he knocked and went into hiding. When the servant came the wise man and the king peered from behind some bushes at what was happening. The servant saw the box, read the paper, and when he shook and heard the clang he shivered, pressed the box against his chest, he looked around and went back into his house. The king and the wise man got closer to the window to see the scene...

The servant threw to the floor everything on the table leaving only the candle. He sat down and emptied the contents of the box... their eyes could not believe what they were seeing.

It was a mountain of gold coins! He, had never touched one of these coins, now had a mountain of them! The servant would touch them and piled them up, caressing them and making them shine at the light of the candle. He would piled them and then spilled them, making piles of coins. So, playing and playing he began making piles of 10 coins. One of ten, two piles of ten, three piles, four, five, and six while totaling 10, 20, 30, 40, 50, 60... until the last stack formed: 9 coins!!!

His gaze swept the table first, looking for another coin. Then the floor and finally the box.

–   "It can't be," he thought. He put the last pile next to the others and confirmed that the pile was smaller.
–   Robbed Me! - He yelled - they robbed me, yes, they robbed me!

Again he looked at the table, on the floor, in the box, in his clothes, he emptied his pockets, moved the furniture, but did not find what he sought.

On the table, as if mocking him, a glowing mound reminded him that he had 99 gold coins, only 99.

–   "99 coins is a lot of money," he thought. "But I need a coin. Ninety-nine is not a whole number. One Hundred is a full number but ninety nine is not."

The king and his advisor looked through the window. The face of the servant was no longer the same, he was frowning and had stiff features, the eyes had become small and wrinkled and the mouth showed a horrible rictus through which you could see bulged teeth. The servant kept the coins in the box and looking around to see if anyone from the house was looking, he hid the box between the firewood.

Then he took pen and paper and sat down to do calculations. How long would the servant have to save to bring his coin count to one hundred? **Pacing back and forth and speaking to himself, he** thought long and hard about how he could achieve it. Then, perhaps, he would not need to work anymore. With one hundred gold coins a man is rich. With one hundred pieces he can live peacefully. He calculated. If he worked and saved his salary and any extra money he received, in eleven or twelve more years he would gather what was needed. "Twelve years is a long time," he thought.

Maybe he could ask his wife to seek work in the village for a while. And he himself, finishing his work in the palace at five in the afternoon, could work until evening and get some extra pay for it. He did the math: adding his work in the village and his wife's, in seven years he would gather the money.

It was too long!!! Maybe he could take to town what remained of his food and sell it for a few coins. In fact, the less they ate, the more food he would have to sell...sell...sell...

It was hot. Why so many winter clothes? Why more than one pair of shoes? It was a sacrifice, but after four years of sacrifice he would reach the one hundred.

The king and the wise man returned to the palace. The servant had entered circle 99... During the following months the servant kept his plans as planned that night. One morning the servant entered the royal bedchamber knocking on doors, muttering and very angry.

- What's wrong? - Asked the king in a good mood.
- Nothing is happening, nothing is happening.
- Not too long ago, you smiled and sang all the time.
- I do my job. Right? What more does your Highness want? To be your jester and juggler too?
- It was not long before the king dismissed the servant.

It was nice to have a servant that was always cranky."[22]

"Money is a good servant but a bad master," the saying goes. It is excellent to facilitate the development of life, but if we give it preeminence it complicates existence. As a family we have to move forward, we are called to prosper in a significant way, but without entering circle 99.

Bibliography references of this section:

1. Wood, B. (s / f). *Basta el Amor [Love is Enough!]* Argentina: South American Publishing House.

2. Botting, G. (1995). *El Abecedario de la Libertad Financiera [The ABCs of Financial Freedom].* California: Pacific Union Conference.

3. Bustos, H. (1998). *Educación Financiera de la Familia [Family Financial Education].* California.

4. Galatians 6:7.

5. Botting, Op. Cit.

6. Ecclesiastes 5:10.

7. González, O. (1994). *Manual de Finanzas Familiares [Family Finance Manual].* Dominican Republic: Artinpresos.

8. Lancer, P. (2003). *Nuevo Diccionario Enciclopédico Empresarial [New Encyclopedic Dictionary of Business]*. Santo Domingo: Editora University UASD.

9. Perello, C. (2003). *Finanzas Personales [Personal Finance]*. Dominican Republic: Edita - Books, S. A.

10. Dayton, H. (1994). *Su Dinero: ¿Frustración o Libertad? [Your Money: Frustration or Freedom?]* Colombia: Editorial Unilit.

11. Keeffe, C. (1995). *Cómo Obtener lo que Usted Quiere con el Dinero que Tiene [How to Get What You Want with the Money You Have]*. Colombia: Norma Publishing Group.

12. Id., page. 137.

13. Burkett, L. (1990). *La Familia y Sus Finanzas [The Family and Your Finances]*. Michigan: Editorial Spokesperson.

14. Psalm 41:1, 2.

15. Proverbs 19:17.

16. Psalm 24:1, 2.

17. Burkett. Op. Cit.

18. Reid, E. (1995). *Su Dinero y Usted [Your Money and You]*. Colombia: Inter - American Publishing Association.

19. Swindoll, C. (1985). *Dile Que Si al Amor [Say Yes to Love]*. EE. UU.: Editorial Betania.

20. 3 John 2.

21. Luke 12: 15.

22. Medina, O. (2003). *Para Animar un Corazón [To encourage a Heart]*. Dominican Republic: Print The Remnant.

SECTION 4
THE COUPLE AND SEX

CHAPTER 7

---❧---

ENJOY SEXUALITY IN YOUR MARRIAGE

*O*ome young lady was describing to her college friend the type of companion she would like to have. *"I want someone – she would say – with whom to share. A friend is what I want... to be with him and stay together... but always as siblings, no sex."* It goes without saying that it took long for this girl to find someone. Over time, this young woman married and as a result of their union, not long after, conceived "two little brothers." What made her change her mind? Undoubtedly, the fact that she understood that "sexuality is also a dimension of a couple's relationship."[1]

It is understood that in all marital dyad, that could be described as successful, intimacy is not considered a missing element as stated by Dr. Grunlan, quoted by Valenzuela (1997): *"A couple can have good sex without a good marriage, but you cannot have a good marriage without good sex."*[2]

Countless people go into marriage with certain expectations regarding sexuality and in many cases, they remain dissatisfied with the passing of years. Expressions like *"I do not know what an orgasm is!"* Or *"This woman has inhibited sexual desire"* is often heard in and out of therapy clinics.

Trends with Regards to Sexuality

In her lectures on Marriage Preparation, Dr. DePaiva, from the University of Montemorelos, Mexico, expressed to her students that there are several trends with regards to sexuality in existence today. According to what you have learned in your life, each person has adopted any of these trends, which strongly affect everything about their sexual behavior. Consider these trends:

1. ***"Sexuality is something low and degrading, therefore it should be avoided."*** A person who keeps in their mind this concept will feel guilty when participating in intercourse with their partner. They will seem evasive and mostly indisposed. Although they feel they love their partner, they do not want to degrade or be degraded or feel gratified with something *"so low"* as sex.

2. ***"Sexuality is a necessary evil"*** as stated by St. Augustine. Some understand that sexuality is evil, but we cannot live without it, therefore, it is a necessary evil for the human race.

3. ***"Sex is free."*** *"Do it whichever way you want... where ever you want... with whomever you want... as often as you want..."* Sadly this is a concept that has reached high sympathy at this time. Uncensored sex, that gives rein to all sorts of fantasies and also gives free expression to sexual debauchery, is really a type of slavery and not really freedom. This concept was definitely one of the best allies of AIDS and other sexually transmitted diseases.

4. ***"For men only..."*** Although not verbalize, this thought beats in the minds of many men. Culture, education and other factors appear to have transmitted a male figure that reaches a greater expression to the extent with which he achieves his satisfaction and fulfillment at the expense of his consort, applauding this way a hedonist thought.

He conceives that a woman should participate in the sexual act, but always with the idea of pleasing all desires and whims of the husband, although not in accordance with their principles or ideas. Usually, the woman of this husband notices his rush in their intimate relationship and she does not achieve experiencing climax through orgasm.

5.   *"Sexuality is a business."* The public or external business of sexuality is called prostitution. However, the marketing of the body for sexual purposes also occurs internally in the home, as a powerful resource used by many spouses to achieve their purposes.

6.   *"It is a matter of personal interest."* Far from being a form of reciprocating a sublime manifestation of love, sexuality is used this way to achieve some personal purpose that could provide or maintain some satisfaction, such as procreation, status, standard of living, and so on.

7.   *"Sexuality is sacred, a gift of God to man."*[3] A couple that conceives sexuality as sacred, also sees it as something holy, pure and clean separated for a special use and in an exclusive context, marriage. For those who support this trend, sexuality is a gift of God to man in order to make it fully enjoyable by the couple.

Is Sex a Gift?

If sex is a gift, who gave it? For what purpose? The Scriptures show that when Adam and Eve left the hands of the Creator, as part of their gift and blessing, He gave them the interesting indication to be fruitful, multiply and fill the earth... [4] In the entire Bible sex appears in a positive and realistic picture as an integral part of what is matrimonial life.[5]

"Therefore a man shall leave his father and mother and be joined to his wife, and they become one flesh"[6] was another advice received by the first couple at the start of their married career. The author of Hebrews said: *"Marriage is honorable in all, and the bed undefiled..."*[7].

"Let the husband render unto the wife due affection: and likewise also the wife unto the husband" noted Apostol Paul. "The wife hath not power of her own body, but the husband; and likewise the husband hath not power over his own body, but the wife. Defraud ye not one another... "8 he said in his useful recommendations.

According to the divine purpose, reproduction and sexual pleasure were the two basic reasons that accompanied this gift of God given at the beginning. Genesis 1: 27 and 28 provides that sexuality should be monogamous and heterosexual, as "male and female he created them" and also gave them instruction to reproduce.

Therefore, can sex be enjoyed with your partner? Remember that this was one of the original purposes. "Drink waters out of thine own cistern, - says Solomon in Proverbs 5: 15-19 and running waters out of thine own well. Let thy fountains be dispersed abroad, and rivers of waters in the streets. Let them be only thine own, and not strangers' with thee. Let thy fountain be blessed: and rejoice with the wife of thy youth...let her breasts satisfy thee at all times and be thou ravished always with her love."

My Mental Attitude and the Sexual Act

The sexual response of an individual is closely linked to the mindset they might have. The brain is the largest sex organ, not the eyes, ears or genitals. As affirmed by Doctors Aguilar and Galbes (1990) who point out: *"Actually eyes do not see, nor our ears hear; is the brain that sees and hears. The proof is in that a person who has their eye and optic nerve, or ear and the auditory nerve in perfect condition, if they suffer a brain injury in the relevant area, they will not see or hear... So we talk with authority when we say that the main sex organ is the brain."*[9]

What we were taught in our house, patterns shaped by our parents in their capacity as a couple, labels or nicknames assigned in childhood, what we have heard from others, the contribution of our cultural environment as well as our own past event, shape or design the layout of our thoughts and structure our attitude about sex.

An orientation influenced by one or more negative experiences, foreign or personal, can cause severe psychological injuries that reduce or inhibit sexual desire in an individual. The same anorgasmia, or sexual dysfunction that affects women is associated in many cases to traditions or stories, such as taboos about sex that were assimilated during childhood and adolescence. Moreover, the prominent sexologist Dinzey Rosa believes that *"sex is different for men and women. Woman give sex to get love, while men give love to get sex."*[10]

So, if sexual activity is experienced as "sin" or "task", it will not contribute to the general welfare, but rather can bring problems and complaints. On the contrary, if it is recognized as a space of coming together, of enjoyment, of giving yourself, of mutual and shared affection, the sexual intimacy becomes playful, erotic and entertaining, and it thus becomes an element of growth for the couple and for each member individually.

Sex is not just a physical act, it also involves emotions, intellect and spirit. Seen from the biological aspect is a way to release stress, but beyond this, is a *"giving"* yourself completely, where the aforementioned elements are unified with the only purpose of providing full enjoyment to the beloved.

An open and healthy mindset further understands that sex is not everything in a relationship, but that love reciprocated in its "give and take" does not, unnecessarily, allow the postponement of its intimacy. Rather, leads them to unequivocally fuse, giving way to the rebirth, every time, of newer and better emotions. In this case, aside from the full enjoyment of the relationship, they achieve other important benefits in matters of health. *"New research shows that the pleasure in bed prevents heart attacks, fights depression, prevents cellulite, improves memory and helps rejuvenate."* Said the surgeon and sex therapist Maria Hurtado, citing a study.[11]

Sexual human activity, according to the design of its Inventor is the result of a close monogamous heterosexual relationship between two people in love, whose main interest is to achieve complete satisfaction of your partner.

Positions in the Bedroom

In order for sexual intimacy to be truly pleasing for the couple, both have to be in complete agreement, in its implementation and how to carry it out. Often, variations in the form of *"making love"* will add a tone that can be very attractive, if enjoyment is increased. Some say that there are over 400 positions for sexual intercourse; others, like Legman (cited by McCary) mentions the existence of up to just over 14 million variations.[12] however, performing many of them may require the partners to be good acrobats.

There are positions that turn out to be more enjoyable than others; some may be unpleasant. In any case, it is desirable that the position be truly comfortable for both. There are 4 positions that are considered fundamental, then, a number of variations of these. For the purposes of this chapter we will address these four fundamental positions:

1. *Face to face or the **"missionary position"**,* the man being on top. This is the most commonly used position in society. In this one, the man takes over in the sexual act.

2. *Face to face the woman being on top, also known as the **"missionary"** position.* This mode offers women an excellent opportunity to express their sexuality, becoming a more active agent.

3. ***Face to face, lateral.*** Favorably in cases of obesity, fatigue, illness or dissimilar heights.

4. ***Vaginal penetration from behind.*** Basically in a lying down position, this position is very useful for those who go through convalescence, advanced pregnancy or seniors, for its convenience and the restful results. At the same time, it is clear that the introduction of the penis is not always easy.[13]

CHAPTER 8

✦

MAKING THE SEXUAL ACT A MORE INTERESTING EVENT

*T*he next topic addresses the questions: What women expect from their husbands before, during and after sex? And, what men expect from their wives before, during and after sex? The answers presented below were found in the research we did among Hispanic groups in the United States. It covers from 2004 to 2014. We had participation of 200 couples from different countries including: Mexico, Guatemala, El Salvador, Puerto Rico, Cuba, Dominican Republic, Honduras, Colombia, Ecuador and Peru. This research realizes the significant differences between male and female to express what their expectations in the art of love are.

What Women Expect from their Husbands Before, During and After Sex?

Gathered in working groups to develop workshops on Human Sexuality, women were asked, what were those things they wanted their husbands to do before, during or after intercourse. They expressed their preferences for these three important moments of intimacy:

Before the Sexual Act:

- Good treatment during the day.

- Get involved with her in some of the household chores.

- Good communication.

- Hygiene and rich smells (good from afar and up close).

- That he sends revealing signals of his masculine intention.

- Bathing together.

- From time to time, surprising her with a gift, maybe some underwear he would like her to use.

- The chosen site to be cozy and sometimes varied.

- Glimmering light, romantic atmosphere.

- Physical touch, caresses and foreplay.

- Abundant creativity.

During the Sexual Act:

- Listening to an "I love you" and other similar words.

- Slow... For him to take his time to explore her entire body.

- The use of motivating music, instrumental or other pleasant music

- To compliment her using kind and delicate words.

- "To wait for her..."

- To avoid any possible distractions.

- Use of different positions.

- To tell her what he is feeling.

- To make sure that she is left satisfied.

After the Sexual Act:

- To remain cuddled.

- "Please do not turn your back."

- Kissing of the buttocks.

- Some groups agreed for there to be a second "run at it" if he can.

- Not to fall asleep immediately after.

- To give thanks.

- Talk about beautiful things.

- To occasionally ask, "Honey, on a scale of 1 to 10, how was I?"

- To shower or Jacuzzi together.

What Men expect from their Wives Before, During and After Sex Act?

In the study cited above, which involved 200 separate couples from different countries, men revealed these were their preferences indicating what they wanted from their wives during the three most important moments of the intimate act:

Before the Sexual Act:

- To dress up with very little clothing suitable for the occasion.

- Occasionally, for her to take the initiative.

- Avoid unpleasant subjects.

- Cell phones off.

- Lit Hearts.

- Massages.

- A good grooming, on occasions, doing it together.

- Prepare the home environment and/or room.

- For the children to be sleeping.

- To use candles, possibly aromatics.

During the Sexual Act:

- To be active in the act.

- To use expressiveness and spontaneity.

- Concentrate on the act.

- For her to say what she likes and dislikes.

- Expressions of affection such as kissing and caresses.

- Appropriate music.

- Use different sex games.

After the Sexual Act:

- If she likes it, to express it.

- If possible, to repeat it.

- Stay a while in bed.

- Caresses and kisses.

- Mutual hygiene.

- Drink a fresh juice or other beverage.

- To let him sleep.

Techniques and Games in the Art of Loving:

For the art of loving to be truly an art it must be more than romantic. Associating it to sexuality, a teacher said *"who in their work only use hands: they are laborers ... those who only use their hands and mind: they are craftsmen, but those who use their hands, mind and heart: those are real artists.* "[14]

Many husbands fail at the moment of intimacy because they manifest an inclination of unmeasured anxiousness in reaching an orgasm, rushing their partner, instead of giving them loving treatment during the day; to please and meet their needs or desires without there being a reward or gratification. Similar to the Renaissance period, today many prefer the discouraged style of "orienting their sexuality towards hedonism," the pursuit of pleasure and self-centeredness[15] as a way to expand their power.

Each couple has a latent ability to develop the art of loving, although it is noteworthy that none are born with an integrated precise instruction manual to achieve the top. Take into account that in the interest of achieving their orgasm they each have different functions.

Smalley and Trent say that men are like a microwave oven, ready to fire at any time, while women are like a crock pot, they need to simmer in order to fully experience sex.[16]

Therefore, a phone call with sexual innuendo would be useful, beautiful and rewarding words, motivating her mental preparation as well as some touches and preparatory games when you get home. The women's entire body is highly sensitive to touch. In particular, caressing the erogenous zones: neck, breasts, front and rear sides of the buttocks and genital area, including indirectly touching the adjacent sides of the clitoris, to avoid pain or discomfort. This will produce a special pleasure and will get her ready for penetration. *"The use of foreplay facilitates the enjoyment longed by woman, while her own husband will reach his climax."*[17]

Patience will be a very important factor in achieving orgasm. Some wives might need 20 to 45 minutes, longer in some circumstances, to reach what a man would easily reach in just a few minutes. Meanwhile, if properly and continuously stimulated *"a woman can have up to six or more orgasms in a single sexual activity, not men, who only between 6 and 8% manage to achieve more than one orgasm in each sexual experience, usually if they are young."*[18]

As for the sexual response, researchers William H. Masters and Virginia E. Johnson in 1966 offered and important contribution to the field of sexuality, with the known longitudinal study that bears their name. The same was done with 10 thousand people, analyzing the reactions of individuals in the sexual act. They found that the response to sexual act is divided into the following phases: excitement, plateau, orgasm and resolution.

The excitation is produced by necking, petting throughout the body and sex play. In men, the first sign of arousal is a penile erection, which occurs in a few seconds, if not sooner, before you begin petting. In the case of women vaginal lubrication can occur about ten seconds after she has started her sexual excitement sexual.[19]

"If sexual stimulation continues to be effective, you reach the peak of excitement, and then passes to the plateau phase. This is a transitional phase until it reaches the threshold, which triggers orgasm."[20] which is the pleasant and compulsive response of the nervous system to sexual stimuli received. After the orgasm is the resolution phase or refractory period in which the sexual organs return to their flaccid state.

CHAPTER 9

✦

SEXUAL ADJUSTMENT AND ENJOYMENT IN DIFFERENT CIRCUMSTANCES

*T*he sexual fit of a partner may not always be expected on the first night of their honeymoon. Although it is certainly possible to achieve in your relational process, usually, it is a common good that requires a definite purpose and dedication from both, as well as patience, adequate communication and time.

Any couple who has a sufficient interest in improving their sexual relationship will achieve important and gratifying progress, only if they are able to communicate what their frustrations and needs are. The co-participation of what makes them enjoy and the good disposition to implement such details can unleash the fire in their bedroom.

There are, however, some elements that exert a strong negative influence, preventing or limiting to a significant degree for the couple to reach an adequate level of rapport and sexual adjustment. Among those we cite:

1. Frequent and severe marital conflicts.
2. Inadequate mental attitude about sex, motivated by issues of formation or unpleasant past experiences.
3. Not letting your spouse know what you like and dislike during the sexual act.
4. Give an impression of enjoyment, while maintaining silence and hiding your true feelings.

5.   Having an environment with little privacy or regular interruptions.

6.   Only interested in achieving your own pleasure and not be interested in the enjoyment of the other.

7.   Consider sex as an element of punishment or reward.

8.   Require the other to do what they understand they should not or do not want to.

9.   Belittle your consort by their condition, whether gender-related changes in physical morphology, among others.

10.   Doubting the true love of a spouse or have distrust of the loyalty of your partner.

11.   Having your partner and thinking of a third party.

12.   Depending on pornographic projections to experience orgasm with your spouse.

13.   Repressed feelings toward a spouse, such as: not forgiven or forgotten errors, anger, hate, old wounds and others.

14.   The presence of sexual dysfunction in one of the partners.

15.   When certain hormonal problems appear.

16.   The use of certain medications that cause side effects.

17.   Have been sexually abused during childhood, abuses still unresolved.

18.   Drug addiction and alcoholism.

19.   The presence of certain psychological problems "such as depression, anxiety disorders, anxiety, personality problems, adjustment reactions, neurosis, etc."

20.   The disuse of appropriate techniques in the art of love making.

21.   Freedom or *"permission"* to say *"not tonight my love"* and be understood or comprehended.

What Happened to my Partner?

Few things are as catastrophic in the life of a man as recognition of any sexual incompetence. Because of their gender, men tend to auto regard himself as a lion in this field. The figure of lion also known as *"King of the Jungle"* comes in part from his great sexual prowess. Merino, quoted by Aguilar and Galbes mentions that "the thrust of a lion knows no brake, and nothing stops it when it has been accepted by a female. He can mate with the lioness during heat, every 21 minutes, i.e. more than fifty times in two days."[21]

If a man feels the presence of an abnormality that prevents him from having a good sexual response, he should see the corresponding doctor in order to eliminate the cause and find a solution. *Some studies indicate that about 50% of sexual problems are caused by hormonal changes, which can be solved with specific treatments.* Such is the case of thyroid disease, diabetes and others. Sexologists, as Nancy Franjul, have found that this is more common after 50 years of age. Many women who are said to have dysfunction of arousal, organically they are not. This is affirmed by doctors Smalley and Trent when they estimate that *"less than three percent of women are organically frigid"*[22] or sexually uninhibited.

Most causes of dysfunction of male and female arousal are associated with emotional and spiritual causes such as: guilt, grief, anger, fear and depression. Even anomalies such as dyspareunia, which is just genital pain before or after intercourse, and is more common in women who have been raped, such as vaginismus or involuntary spasm of the outer third of the vagina, preventing insertion of the penis, which could be a symptom of mental disorder.

Other "multiple studies on sexual behavior of men and women between 50 and 100 years of age have shown that healthy people 70 years of age, in 70% of cases, are sexually active and have sex regularly, one or more times per week. Kinsey in 1984; Masters and Johnson between 1966 and 1991, Duke between 1953 and 1991 and Starr - Weiner in 1981 give account of it."[23]

However, becoming impotent is a great secret fear suffered by much of the male population, because if that is the case he understands that his manhood would be severely threatened. This *"male epidemic"* can implicate importance in the moral, psychological and legal order. *"In some countries sexual impotence is grounds for divorce and the Catholic Church considers the condition as an important factor in the process of annulment."*[24]

According to a study by the University of Boston, USA, *"up to 52% of men, who are between 40 and 70 years of age, today suffer from some form of sexual dysfunction that prevents them from achieving penile erection and maintain it for the time necessary to normally consummate the sexual act."*[25]

Fortunately, we can say that erectile dysfunction is no longer a devastating problem in most cases. Low self-esteem, along with the inability to achieve enjoyment in the bedroom and premature ejaculation, may be issues of the past if we do more than suffer in silence. Visiting the doctor or sex therapist, having the appropriate studies done and continuing the treatments that are indicated, could mean the difference.

The Sex Act during Pregnancy

Pregnancy is a very essential step in the life of every woman; full of joy, fears and myths, especially if this is the first occasion. Usually the couple experiment with some changes during this stage. Many women may feel tired or have other ailments, such as a case of nausea, vomiting, etc., which usually occurs in the first quarter.

In the second trimester, when there is a better degree of adaptation to the pregnancy, sex can achieve a freer expression of fears, even being enjoyed by some more than ever before! By the third quarter there is a remarkable growth of the belly which tends to be a barrier between the members of the couple.

However, a lot of couples, up to 75% continued with their sexual activities on a regular basis, as revealed by some studies.[26]

During pregnancy sex can be more spontaneous and even relaxed, especially amongst those couples who had been trying pregnancy through treatments. You no longer keep track of dates, pills, etc. *"Sexual activity in this period can help prepare the muscles for vaginal delivery."*[27]

It is important, that the couple talk about ways they would like or could show love, being more romantic, although sometimes, due to discomforts caused by pregnancy, it does not necessarily have to end with penetration. Some positions that could be recommended during pregnancy are the woman on top, or both on your side and vaginal penetration from behind.

Some ladies expressed fears of the loss of her pregnancy because of sex. So far there is no scientific evidence showing any truth to justify this fear. However, there are cases in which the intimate act would be unwise, if the doctor thinks it appropriate.

Sex during pregnancy could be interrupted in cases of: threat of abortion or vaginal bleeding. Also in the case of premature plac enta, or if there is a vaginal infection. In such cases, there should be communication with your obstetrician. Similarly, the appearance of abdominal cramps, severe pain, premature birth or a multiple pregnancy, among others, are certainly events that indicate the need for suspension of sexual activities.

Sexuality during the Tertiary Age

Some believe that after sixty there is a decrease in sexual desire. The experience of many who have exceeded this age limit, say that on the contrary, this could be the best stage of life to enjoy sex. In the time in which we live, advances in science, a good diet and frequent exercise are factors that influence people to live longer, maintaining good overall health.

Our memories and feelings are in tact as well as desires that are inherent to human beings. Despite this, there may be special health conditions that make it difficult, during this period or even impossible, for sexual activity during this stage of life and as a result the interest or desire to share with your partner is eliminated.

It should be stressed that it is very possible that significant physical changes are becoming notable, such as body volume and the way we carry ourselves, hair color, among others. However, it is interesting to remember that this is the same person you married. Despite external changes, inside of that person is something admirable which are values and those beautiful qualities that will make one even more precious after the passing of time and that go beyond the physical attractiveness.

Spouses who have cultivated good communication during the early years of their marriage and have stable health, will find yet more reasons to have a good intimate relationship. If you had quality sex when you were a young couple, it is very likely that in adulthood, when the nest is now empty, the relationship will continue with remarkable sparks.

"Even at age 95 about 40% of people were interested in sex," cites a study published by a Cuban medical journal. It reports that *"in 1994 in a group of people over 70 years of age, 81% of those married, remained sexually active."*[28]

Similarly, a significant number of elderly patients do not participate in sex due to elements such as *"increasing age, female gender and widowhood, the presence of some diseases (hypertension, heart disease, etc.). There are also other associated factors, such as deterioration of the marriage relationship, lack of privacy and sexual dysfunctions."*[29]

One advantage of geriatric sexuality is that women do not have to fear getting pregnant,[30] which can enhance your relaxation. However, while women no longer have their reproductive capacity in no way have they lost their capacity to love.

No matter the couples age, with regards to their sexual activity it would always be good to formulate the following six questions: Is my sexual practice performed in a positive way? Is it relaxing? Can I consider it pleasant? Is it romantic? Is it physically satisfying? Is it emotionally satisfying? Obviously, the best answer expected is an affirmative one and at the same time it is the biggest and achievable challenge.

Bibliography references of this section:

1.   Cáceres, J. (1997). *10 Palabras Clave Acerca de la Pareja [10 Key Words About the Couple]*. Argentina: Piados.

2.   Valenzuela. , A. (1996). *Casados, Pero Contentos [Married, But Conte Happy]*. Michigan: Promise Productios.

3.   Course Notes. (1999). *Preparación para el Matrimonio [Preparation for Marriage]*. Masters in Family Relations. University of Montemorelos, Mexico. UM: Extension Dominican Republic.

4.   Genesis 1: 28.

5.   Taylor, G. (1983). *La Familia Auténtica Cristiana [Authentically the Christian Family]*. Michigan: Editorial Spokesperson.

6.   Genesis 2:24.

7.   Hebrews 13:4.

8.   1 Corinthians 7:3-4.

9.   Aguilar, I. and Galbes, H. (1990). *Enciclopedia Familiar Vida, Amor y Sexo [Family Life Enciclopedia, Love & Sex]*. 2nd. Edition, Volume 1. Spain: Editorial Safeliz.

10. Interview with Dr. Roza Dinzey in July, 2004. Dominican Republic.

11. More information: http://www.salud.pontecool.com/zoom.php?tip=62

12. McCary, J. et al, (1996). *Sexualidad Humana de McCary, [McCary Human Sexuality]*, 5th. Edition. Mexico: Editorial El Manual Moderno [Editorial Modern Manual].

13. Course notes: *Dinámicas de la Sexualidad Humana [Dynamics of Human Sexuality]*. Master of Family Relations. University of Montemorelos, Mexico.

14. Quote of Dr. Neptalí Miranda, used in the course: *Estudio Científico de la Familia [Scientific Study of the Famil]*. Master of Family Relations. University of Montemorelos, Mexico.

15. Liscano, J. (1988). *Los Mitos de la Sexualidad en Oriente y Occidente [Myths of Sexuality in East and West]*. Spain: Editorial Laia, Alfadil Editions.

16. Smalley, G. and Trent, J. (1990). *El Amor es una Decisión [Love is a Decision]*. USA: Editorial Caribe.

17. LaHaye, T. (1990). *El Acto Matrimonia [The Marriage Act]*. Spain: Editorial CLIE.

18. McCary. Op. Cit, p. 172.

19. Wheat, E. (1980). *El Placer Sexual Ordenado por Dios [Sexual Pleasure Ordered by God]*. USA: Editorial Bethania.

20. Álvarez, J. et al, (1986).*Sexoterapia Integral [Integral Sex Therapy]*. Mexico: Editorial El Manual Moderno.

21. Op cit. *Enciclopedia Vida, Amor y Sexo [Life, Love & Sex Encyclopedia]*, Volume 1, p. 248

22.   Op Cit. *Amar es una Decisión [Love Is A Decision]*, p. 65.

23.   More information at: http://www.encolombia.com/medicina/revistas-medicas/menopausia/vol-2196/vivencias_sexualidad_condiciones_meno2-1/

24.   Lescault, A. (s/f). *Problemas Sexuales del Hombre [Male Sexual Problems]*. Mexico: Family Institute, Editorial Concepts, Inc.

25.   Id.

26.   More information at: http://www.babysitio.com/embarazo/sexo_disfrutar.php

27.   More information at: http: //www.bvs.sld.cu/revistas/mgi/vol_18_5_02/ 27. mgi0852002.html

28.   Id.

29.   Rus, A. (1997). *El Sexo de la A a la Z Para Gente Joven [Sex from A to Z For Young People]*. Spain: Ediciones Temas de Hoy.

30.   Wheat, E. (1984). *El Amor Que no se Apaga [The Inextinguishable Love]*. USA: Editorial Bethania.

THE COUPLE: CRISIS AND OPPORTUNITIES

CHAPTER 10

MANIFESTATION AND ORIGIN OF CONFLICT

*A*t any given time, all couples go through some type of conflict. Sometimes they are problems that are common to any family, but other times, they are serious issues that require special attention. This may occur in any or all of their life cycles, for that reason, consciousness of it motivates us to be better prepared.

Throughout all phases of our marital relationships, we can all somehow find ourselves in a situation worthy to be called "a fight." Given this reality, the most important thing is not fighting it is to achieve relief, and to do it so that it is helpful.

The couple already has a varied number of matters which by their nature cause concern: Payment of rent or mortgage, children's school fees, unforeseen situations , a family member's illness, labor issues or lack of it, amongst many other things. If in addition to all this, we make our home a boxing stadium, because of small differences that occurred sometimes due to unimportant things, then you are depriving the family of those pleasant moments that add meaning to the system. The children who observe these episodes are usually not very obedient, but tend to imitate.

Manifestations and Reactions upon Conflict

A conflict is an unsolved problem accentuated if you are not paying attention. Taught by our environment, some call it litigation, tantrum, mess, marital conflicts and crisis amongst other things. Dr. Youngberg says *"A crisis is a turning point. It is a time of return for an individual, family or group".*[1]

This word, "crisis", comes from the Greek vocabulary Krinein that means deciding,[2] which treated in the correct way, is an excellent opportunity to grow and strengthen family bonds. It can be used to prepare us for a future crisis. Family conflicts occur frequently in many homes and in many ways.

How do members of a couple resolve conflicts? Usually, the way their parents did. Some manifest themselves verbally, using phrases so hurtful that they poison the relationship and as an excuse simply say "I have no hair on my tongue." Others express conflict through domestic violence.

There are also those who prefer to discuss their differences in a personal or private manner; are intentional in terms of seeking solutions and show a real commitment. On the other hand, there are those who do not care to display their differences openly, without fear of the natural consequences of this action.

Hybels (1994), presents four common reactions that lead individuals to conflict:

- **"Freeze them."** In this case, everyone in the home knows that we have a problem. But there is an attitude of isolation because nobody dares to approach it, hoping that time itself will *"thaws it"*.

- **"Shoot the bullets."** The couple lives here, as if filming a *"cowboys"* movie. Anything that bothers them is a powerful motive to shoot deadly phrases. They yell, they hurt each other, throw objects, damage their property, they harm themselves, but above all their own children.

- **"Get me out of here."** Many prefer to flee. They hide behind the false solutions offered by drugs or alcohol. Once drunk or stoned they feel *"liberated"*. Sometimes the person promises they will leave the house, and for a while they do. Then they return quiet, they no longer drink and everything seems fine, although they do not address the problem. What is happening? Problems are never resolved because they are never faced, therefore, at the next conflict we will see this same episode being repeated.

- ***"I do not know what happened."***[3] Unfortunately, some people react to conflicts inflicting abuse on their family members. They possibly learned this with sorrow and tears within their own household. Although they promised themselves that they would do better than their parents did, when trouble occurs, when anger makes them react like an erupting volcano, what do they do, exactly what they have learned? They beat, abuse and then complain saying they do not know why it happened. Usually, the reaction arises almost spontaneously, unless it has received adequate treatment to properly help channel their negative feelings and emotions.

The effect of marital conflict is also expressed through continuous complaints and lamentations that fill the homes atmosphere with discontent. Some take it in silence, accumulating tension, but feel impotent. Therefore, choosing to ignore the situation without any reduction in its enormous emotional burden, to the point of triggering a physical or psychological problem, or a separation or divorce.

Why do Marital Conflicts Occur?

What are the real causes that can be hidden behind a marital conflict? In general, the existence of this can be motivated by endogenous or exogenous sources. Let's look at these two elements in more detail:

Endogenous Factors: Causes that originate within the person, such as an illness, guilt, anxiety, fear, resentment, different policies and so on.

They range from normal female cycle, situations that cause variation in the mood, to the reactions caused by the use of certain drugs, in cases of certain health conditions. We can cite:

- Diabetes
- Thyroids
- Depression
- Temperament
- Menstruation
- Nervous maladjustments
- Among others

The physical condition itself and/or any irregularity in the emotional field, as a result of an important event or significant deficiency, can result in behavior that leads to conflict in the family. It is not the same as having a healthy physical condition to having pains in your body, spending the whole night without sleep and rely on the use of drugs for life. Nor is it the same as having a mind in stable emotional condition than suffer from depression, anxiety, panic or live with feelings of anger, bitterness and resentment among others.

Exogenous Factors: The origin of this is found outside the body, amidst such as: culture, environment and other situations in the external order. Exogenous factors can motivate varied conflicts. Among which we can cite:

- Family matters, such as: Birth order, patterns of family formation, the *"marriage license"* and issues of cultural differences.

- Also, here we can include certain situations, such as: poor communication, finances, sexual imbalances, parenting or matters related thereto, religion, personal preferences, and others.

For the convenience of our readers, many of these points are being considered in other chapters of this book.

CHAPTER 11

HOW DOES BIRTH ORDER INFLUENCE BEHAVIOR?

One of the most notable specialists in the field of family therapy was Murray Bowen. A doctor and psychiatrist who later devoted great efforts to mental health and who developed the theory that bears his name, which includes the appearance of birth order and its relationship to behavior. Bowen conducted numerous studies on this issue and on several occasions stated to the therapists that *"No single data is more important than knowing the position of people in the order of brothers, in the present and past generations."*[4]

The position you occupy in birth order among your brethren, as well as your gender, influence in a very special way in how you deal with other people. Your status as spouse, parent, friend, employee or employer are clearly affected by the aforementioned reason.

It should be noted, however, that the information herewith given is not a mathematical rule, but it can help you better understand the elements that in many cases characterize each condition. This will explain many of the behaviors that you have been observing in your family relationship, it will also help you to better accept yourself or, in some cases, you may see the need to make important changes.

Is important to say that there are conditions that may vary the characteristics presented below and if they are not adjusted, even alter the way this influences the position in the family. Henríquez and Espaillat (2002) consider that among these conditions we could cite: the small age difference between siblings and the next oldest or youngest, the occurrence of certain special circumstances, such as: change of residence, family separation or death, personal illness, especially physical attractiveness of one of the members, characteristics of physical constitution of a person or special talents, outside family context, and others.

According to Toma (cited by Henriquez and Espaillat) are ten basic types identified in the position of siblings. Other authors add another two, which are included in the list below. Each of these has their own peculiarities that allows individuals to manifest them according to their specific forms. Birth orders are:

1. The oldest brother of brothers

2. The youngest brother of brothers

3. The oldest brother of sisters

4. The youngest brother of sisters

5. The only son

6. The oldest sister of sisters

7. The youngest sisters of sisters

8. The oldest sister of brothers

9. The youngest sister of brothers

10. The only daughter[5]

11. The middle child

12. The twin child

Let us briefly consider the personal characteristics of each of these positions, including also the middle children and twins. Let us observe how they influence your character, your social and marital life.

1. ***The oldest brother of brothers.*** The first child usually is highly desired. Many parents qualify it as their first love, but this is a unique experience. The father identifies with him so much so that sometimes he wants to make him a copy of himself, frequently he is given the same name as the father and he is motivated to walk the same path.

The oldest son among the brothers is used to make many decisions. In the absence of their parents he has to provide solutions to many of the problems that arise at home. So he likes to lead and assume responsibility, but does not like to be criticized. He takes care of men and can be the boss of them. He is usually very fond of those younger than him and tries to help them.

As he had no sisters, he did not have intimate relationship with women. So he is timid in his relationship with the opposite sex. He feels pleased to see that a woman has more interest in him than he for her. Although he can easily treat a woman like a man, he dislikes any masculine appearance she may have. His most convenient companion would be the younger sister of brothers. If he married the older sister of sisters, his home could turn, without much difficulty, into a boxing ring. Normally he is a responsible father and a good provider that shows true concern for his children.

2. ***The youngest brother of brothers.*** Very often the youngest child is the one the mother spoils. "This child is often stubborn, moody, and often rebellious. Although eager for freedom, he is disoriented because he has no structure against which to rebel, and it is possible he is very dependent on others."[6]

Although highly protected by both parents, everyone bossed him around. In his childhood he had little opportunity to express directly and frankly his feelings of anger, rage and frustration, especially when it came to facing his older brother. Because of that he easily screams and kicks. If he is an adult, when he realizes that he can lose, he just leaves things as they are.

He likes to have many friends and be loved and respected by them. He does not like to be in front because he does not feel prepared to be the decision maker. He likes diversion and living comfortably. He can easily fall into debt. He wants and tries to get things although not always knowing where the money would come from. He likes for everything he does to go well, he is willing to sacrifice himself, but if he fails he tends to feel depressed. With the opposite sex he is obliging, generous and usually treats her well.

If he marries a woman who is an only child or the youngest daughter of sisters, he may be exposed to many conflicts. In truth, he does not understand women well, but his best combination could be the older sister of brothers. If she is understanding and tries to help him, without doing exhibitions for it, he will let her guide him and she could accomplish a lot.

3. ***The oldest brother of sisters.*** This gentleman has something interesting: he does not get along well with men, unless it is another older brother of sisters. Instead he is the man of the women, except with the older sister of sisters, he nurtures them, treats them well, is courteous and considerate. Usually he is also a good administrator. He likes quality of work, he is realistic and not a tyrant. If he must change workplace, he has no difficulty doing so. If he was *"spoiled"* by his mother or his sisters, most likely he expects his friends or spouse, if any, to do the same.

Fortunately, this gentleman would provide a stable marriage with almost all birth orders of the opposite sex. The most appealing combination, however, is the younger sister of brothers, because she is a mold closer to his own. What would happen if he married the oldest daughter of brothers? Since she has spent her life crossing lines downwards, she will try to keep doing that, but with someone whose habit is to do exactly the same. So then, who would be the head of the home? Who will tell the children what to do?

However, with all of this it is possible for them to achieve a good level of refinement. If this man has for a wife an only daughter, they could form a very acceptable couple. He would take care of her with more devotion than many other men and she would feel grateful. The larger the number of sisters he has had and the greater the closeness with his mother, the closer he will be with his wife and children.

4.   ***The youngest brother of sisters.*** When a man is the younger brother of a group of sisters, in the house everyone protects him. He feels happy to be the favored one by his parents above his sisters. Almost always he conforms less to the rules imposed because usually, he is the one with less imposed discipline or punishment. Maybe that is why he never took seriously the few rebukes he received. Consequently, he tends to delay things a lot, he may often be late for commitments and is undisciplined.

With his attitude he can pretend that everyone conforms to him. But his sisters love him a lot, they take good care of him. It is said that this man is the best kind towards women. He is attentive and careful with them. Possibly, his best partner may be the older sister of brothers, who with her maternal style would show him a greater understanding than, for example, the oldest sister of sisters. He does not hurry in life, everything is done at his own pace and engaged in his own limits.

5. ***The only son.*** The only child enjoys greater privileges than only daughters. He is applauded, the wise child, the protected, the good one and even the better one. He wishes and expects the same tribute from others outside the family circle. The truth is that sometimes he has problems with this. Since he had no brothers or sisters, everything was for him. He tends to be *"wasteful"* and has no experience sharing, although he can learn it.

He will seek among woman for the one that will admire him, who will praise him and stands ready to reproduce in his favor the pattern cited above. A woman who is the older sister between sisters or the older among brothers could be a good partner for him, the same as a lady that is a few years older than him. An only child as a companion would be difficult for him, since she would maintained a tough competition for the same place.

Remarkably, this man has been accustomed to having everything done for him, he is helped with things, doing what he wants, how he wants it and when he wants it. Therefore, most likely his habit was to be alone. This can foster a feeling of not being unable to develop a good couple relationship. Often left alone in life. Whomever is the wife of the only son gentleman will notice that he did not learn to be very communicative. But if his wife helps in making his life easier, without requiring him to give more than he can give, they will find a good fit in their relationship.

6. ***The oldest sister of sisters.*** Loves giving orders, pass judgment and have everything under control. She is busy and has a strong character. Since she rest very little, those near her have little leeway. Often this young lady does not have a good time. Why? Because she is mostly feared than loved.

Men call her *"the iron lady"*, considering her difficult to be conquered, although in her opinion, that is not true. Her younger sister competes with her as she is complimented or if she feels displaced. Does not get along with the older sister of brothers and her best mate could be the younger brother of sisters. In the described situation, she would be happy with *"a man accustomed to women who are responsible for making decisions."* An only son or a younger brother of sisters could also be a good match for her. Also, if the younger brother of sisters or only child (as his probable partner) coincides in position with the order or position held by her father, for her would be fantastic.

7. ***The youngest sister of sisters.*** This one states that she needs someone to lead her, guide her. Even as an adult, she will always behave like the younger sister. She is active, sometimes a bit impulsive, very spontaneous, has accents of joy and good humor. Other times she is a bit sloppy in her personal appearance. Some consider her too spoiled, and if she notices that she is being handled she reacts with embarrassment or stubbornness.

Looking to stand out, perhaps she identifies with the oldest and almost certainly will not succeed. For this reason, it is possible that she will try to be her opponent in conduct this way others will look and listen to her. She is risky and brave, appreciates changes, challenges and is motivated to compete. This little lady is usually feminine, flirty, whimsical and dominant. She is good attracting men. Whether it is provoked or not, if she sees that they quarrel or fight over her, she simply enjoys it.

Almost always gets married before the oldest or is sexually active before her. But since she likes change, her relationships are sometimes short-lived. The previous experience an older brother of sisters can make someone of this order a good husband for her. If she marries the older brother of brothers, she could become very dependent on him. Middle sons or an only son also represent a good order, especially if the latter is a bit older than her or if her father was an elder son.

8.   *The oldest sister of brothers.* Is an excellent caretaker of men. She is characterized by her independent spirit, wisdom and strength. She seems to be no less than a *"super woman."* Hardly feels discouraged by conflicting or divergent positions, but the rejection by men or loneliness cause her great harm.

Normally, this lady does not care much for women, instead she gets along well with men. The more brothers, the more she enjoys masculine company. Although she is not the fascination of men, he who has her as companion most likely will be awarded with someone who will support him, being willing, even to leave aside important things like her job, to care for his needs without being demanding. If she had many brothers, is probable it will take long for her to marry or difficult to choose a man. Sometimes she just prefers to be surrounded by them and she enjoys it.

The younger brother of sisters can be a great option for her, as well as a younger brother of brothers. For the latter she could be too dominant and sometimes it happens that he would want to rebel because he feels he cannot find his space.

9.   *The youngest sister of brothers.* As a woman, she has qualities of great brilliance that attract the attention of men: is feminine, attractive, makes friends easily, and is recognized as an affectionate girl, with a happy and fun spirit. She is willing to sacrifice herself and surrender to the maximum, but usually gets what she wants from men. Almost without exception, where she arrives, there is a man who admires her. Gentlemen seek her and she is gentle with them, she listens. However, her mate is

more important to her than money itself. If her parents focused more on her older brother and ignored her talents, it is possible she would have kept hatred or resentment for this, to such point of feeling an inexplicable dislike of men or seek to always be in competition with them to show them her value.

Due to her characteristics, she has a great ability to attract men, including married ones, even if they are older than her. The fact that she could be hurt or destroy a marriage is of little consequence to her. She desires to obtain favors and then leave them on the side of the road. *"The more brothers the youngest sister has, the harder it will be for her settle for one man in her life... But if her big brother offered her security she could have a happy marriage and consider her husband as the most valuable treasure."*[8] The older brother of sisters, for his experience in the fine treatment towards women, can be a good match for her.

10. ***The only daughter.*** To a significant degree, the only daughter is dependent on the attention, care and pampering of her parents. It is special, but not so much like an only son, although she receives more care for being a female than if she was male. Expects everyone to appreciate her, to be treated well, if possible, to render her *"reverence."* Easily pretends for everything and everyone adapt to her, but struggles to adapt to their environment.

Even in adulthood usually seeks the counsel of her parents. It could also be, that her mother will choose her partner. She could combine well with an older brother of sisters, for his delicate nature and in his case because he led several women and could understand her better. Another good option for her would be a middle brother, from whom she would accept his leadership, provided he is able to adequately meet her needs.

However, he must remember that, usually, the mother of an

only daughter is part of the baggage of the offspring. She has a high tendency to be faithful as a couple, but if things are not going well at home, does not go far to return to her parents' home. The only daughter can become very dependent on her husband, especially if she was treated as a *"piece of glass"* at home. Otherwise, and usually, is very confident and independent. Does not agree with divorce, because such a thing represents insecurity for her future, although at present time she is not very skilled or responsible in matters relating to home care.

11. ***The middle child.*** To better understand the reality of the middle child, let us place him in a frame of reference. The eldest son is special and highly anticipated because it is the first, the last or third, if any, is special because there will be no more; but, what is the grace of the middle child? What is so special? The birth expectations are no longer the same, the preparations, provision and care, when compared to those given to the first child. Photos of this are scarce in the family album, and the ones that appear reveal that he wore clothes that had been used by the older brothers. Not so with the first or the last. The special case of the middle child is, that they are like a ping pong ball, neither big or small but frequently wanting to be on one side or another. They do not enjoy opportunities or privileges from their big brother, but neither of the considerations of the younger child. Without any gain, he tries to outdo his older brother and with disappointment tries to receive the attention given to the younger brother.

This person usually grows feeling that life owes them something, something that they deserved and was never given to them. Therefore, they believe that life is unfair. As a result, this individual is prone to accumulate a debt of resentment in their heart. This debt may manifest itself later through a destructive behavior, in other words, conveying to their partner and children the treatment received. Since *"everyone owes them"*, *he or she*, usually thinks that they *"owe nothing"*. In other cases, this feeling of merit may manifest in reverse, i.e., *"although I did not receive, I will give so that mine do not suffer what I suffered"*, what would be in this case a constructive merit.

Since nobody is paying them any attention and they have very little encouragement from their parents, they try to develop in some way. Their painstaking effort can lead to problems of anxiety and rebellion. They may even be a good tyrant. Since they are in the middle, when problems arise, they are not inclined one way or the other, in order not to cause conflicts and avoid being harmed. So the middle child tends to be very conciliatory.

Normally, they are good husbands with most of the other positions, perhaps being the most convenient with another person also in the same position. However, sometimes these are people who can keep marital conflict inside, one after another and for a long time, to the point that the situation becomes very complicated. In this case, they must do their part and face difficulties to the extent they arise.

12. **The twin child.** Almost without exception, a pair of twins is a real highlight. If you are notified of who came first, even by a minute, it is very likely that he will assume the role of older brother of the two or in the case where there is one taller or stronger than the other.

Sometimes, the twins are the latest children to arrive and they receive excessive attention, and a lot of love, to the point they becoming spoiled. They are frequently good peers to each other and stimulate each other in studies using healthy competition. If they are twin girls they are less competitive between themselves and their relationships are close and lasting with the whole family.

Most of their activities are done together. In general, they have a very good relationship. But what happens? It can be very challenging for a twin to be separated from their sibling. For this reason some find it difficult to marry. Taking this step is for them to reproduce the relationship that exists with their counterpart, only this does not regularly satisfies their emotional aspect. If from an early age each one had been treated as a unique being, relationships as adults will be characterized by greater harmony and they would have no drawbacks functioning independently.

CHAPTER 12

OTHER EXOGENOUS FACTORS

*T*here are several elements that can be considered exogenous factors that may be related to the emergence of a marital conflict. Among them are: Family patterns and having received or not received "permission" to marry. Consider these aspects in more detail.

The Family Patterns

Every family has a different mold. Therefore each family will mold their children in light of the context of their own models and according to their own pattehrns. It is within the family where children learn how to behave in the world, *"there is their first school, with their parents as teachers, they must learn the lessons that will guide them through life: lessons of respect, obedience, reverence, and self-control. Educational influences of the home are a decisive power for good or for evil."*[9]

What a child learns in school about home, will be considered accurate. However, what is right for a family, not necessarily has to be right for another. Let us cite just a few examples: With married couples, one presses the tube of toothpaste from the bottom, while the other does so from the middle or from the top. While one places the toilet paper roll inward, perhaps the other places it outward. One was disciplined one way, while the other received other types of punishments. One grew at the foot of a military righteousness and at home everything was moving under strict orders and greetings, but the other person was perhaps the daughter of a comedian.

Now, this youngster adapted to live according to the model provided by his family, which has its mold, is attracted by that lady, who comes from another family, and she too was molded in a peculiar way. The challenge now is to make one pattern out of two patterns. This process is possible, but is not free. It has a price. In the process of adaptation, traits of a pattern of another that were deeply rooted in one of the two and could affect the new relationship may develop. That is where it is necessary to have a definite purpose for the relationship, a serious commitment. A good negotiating spirit and a willingness to seek the best for the success of the home, even if they do not fully meet the parameters of my court, will be very appreciated. Not without reason can we say that *"growing is painful,"*[10] but by no means should we stop growing, but rather, we can improve our attitude about what growing implies.

Marriage Permission

Treating Naggy's interesting issue of Contextual Therapy, Disla would teach his students that in any significant marital relationship there are two fundamental components, namely:

1. The ability to assume commitments

2. The capacity to trust

According to this premise, the relationship in which one of you is not ready to assume it's commitments, or is unwilling to trust will lack the vital elements that sustains it. There are also two other basic components:

1. Loyalty

2. Justice

When talking about whether or not you were given permission to marry, we do not refer to whether the wedding was done with the consent of the parents or if they were there on the occasion of the celebration. It is rather whether they will give you the emotional permission to establish this new loyalty. Many parents who attend their daughter's wedding and even make important contributions to it, never gave her permission to get married.[11]

Willi (1993) meanwhile, agrees with Disla noting that *"an important circle of problems is involved in a new relationship with the family of origin, particularly with the parents. Out of fear or guilt, some fail to erect a limit to their parents, to the point that they intrude in the relationship seizing the opportunities presented to them. You come to a fight over possession between the parents and the husband, to a struggle for dependence and separation."*[12]

When children do not *"break their umbilical cord"* upon getting married, they feel that making a turn of attention, with regards to their parents is gravely disrespectful, comparable to a cruel lack of loyalty.

However, it is expected that in the new relationship, the person establishes a condition of husband and wife that requires a mutual loyalty without having third party interference. Take for example the following case applicable to both: The spouse who has not had permission to marry will have boundary issues between his mother and his wife. Though he knows the place that corresponds to each, prefers to assume the attitude of someone living in confusion.

On the one hand is the mother and the other the wife. He is in the middle feeling pulled by both. The mother conceived and raised him but the wife is the mother of his children and the one who sleeps beside him. The mother even expects certain attentions from her son, as if he were still single, she complains saying: *"Look at that, after I sacrificed so much for him, I work so hard... now he leaves me..."* The gentleman, since he is loyal to his mother, feels guilty, for a while he totally or partially forgets about his wife and concentrates his attention on his mother.

Why has it been so difficult to assume his commitment as husband? Because he did not receive the corresponding permission to establish this new loyalty. Many relationship problems lurk unseen conflicts of loyalty that deserves to be studied honestly and conscientiously.

At one point, the situation seems calm, without any dialogue or therapeutic treatment, because the spouse adopted the attitude of neglect, but the situation rises again causing the usual stress and taking the form of a vicious circle. Minuchin (1999) notes that in this case "both are affected by the failure to resolve the situation."[13]

A husband or wife who needs to be *"too"* attentive to his family of origin, especially parents, to the point of disrupting the limits bordering the territory of the couple, is already notable that such a person did not receive permission to marry. Parents should know that when their children establish their home, they need total independence from them as parents. Similarly, the same way we must accept the idea that the mother's role cannot be eliminated, the role and place of the wife or husband should not be touched. These must be friends, colleagues, lovers, confidants. she as wife, will be the only queen of that circle that will be closed to outside influences and where only God and your partner fit.

Other Important Factors

There are also other factors that are extremely important as causal elements of conflict between partners. Some of them are seen in detail. These include:

1. Financial situations

2. Conjugal communication

3. Matters relating to children: time, education, discipline, etc.

4. Matters relating to sexual satisfaction

5. Recreation and use of free time

6. Relationship with in-laws

7. Conjugal infidelity

8. Household work

9. Domestic violence

10. Others

CHAPTER 13

HOW TO FIGHT SUCCESSFULLY

To fight or not to fight? Unfortunately, conflicts have become part of the human experience. So the point here is to consider how to have a meaningful fight. Charles Swindoll, in his book "Say Yes to Love," presents seven valuable rules to have a fight that is really clean and in which both come out as winners:

Rule # 1: *Keep the fight honest*. Avoid lying and manage yourself within the frame of something that if done without effort, may well be considered a naked truth. Promising yourselves, as a couple, to treat each other with mutual respect and to be honest, no matter what happens, and complying with that agreement, will add enough strength to every relationship.

Rule # 2: *Keep the control*. The words expressed in those moments of anger are sometimes deadly weapons that damage even the best relationships. Instead of attacking the person it is preferable to attack the problem with the person. A mature attitude allows us to see that the inappropriate behavior and not the person was what caused us the grievance.

Rule # 3: *Respect the right time*. For this, obviously, both have to decide what the right time is. A quote from Scripture that motivates us to settle disputes promptly and with elegance is: "do not let the sun go down while you are still angry, and do not give the devil a foothold."[14] You will need honesty and respect to discuss the problem. Although perhaps, you may prefer to request for it to be addressed at a more suitable time and place, however, do use this as an evasive action. It is healthy, according to the above quote, for the couple to choose to resolve their differences on the same day they happen.

Rule # 4: *Keep a positive attitude.* What positive solution do you have to offer upon the occurrence of the problem? Instead of criticizing or grumbling, the wise husband or wife should contribute. Offering a positive solution opens the closed hands of your partner and encourages the heart which is already feeling dejected.

Rule # 5: *Act with tact.* This means being careful of the words we say and the tone of voice we use to pronounce them. I understand that this rule is not so easy to apply at times, but the battle against self is the hardest that we have to fight every day.

Rule # 6: *Maintain privacy.* If you really want the fight to be good, do not dare to publicly attack your partner. Remember that the public has nothing to do with what is happening between both of you, nor will they help you solve your problem, they will simply enjoy the *"show."* The problems of the home should be taken care of in the home, not with friends, or neighbors. In the home and the couple will always have better results.

Rule # 7: *Helps to clean the debris.*[15] "Be kind and compassionate to one another, forgiving each other, just as Christ forgave you."[16] To be benign, tender and have a forgiving spirit are the three basic elements to help clear debris before the fight. Certainly, the issue is not whether or not to fight, but how to fight. There is no doubt that these seven suggestions will help.

Tips for Fixing a Marital Conflict

Two notable researches named John Gottman from the University of Washington and Clifford Notarius of the Catholic

University of America, along with a group of collaborators have investigated, for about 20 years, how a couple resolves their conflicts. Based on the findings of their investigation, these specialists agree that *the relationships that achieve robustness differ from the relationships that barely survive or die easily in the way their members face and resolve their conflicts and differences when these arise.*

To resolve conflict some people prefer to ignore it. They resign themselves to a model in which I lose and you lose. With this attitude the conflict grows. Others do not know whether to please or soften a little and take the ambiguous style of losing and let the other win. For those who are more competitive, however, the imperative is to win and see the other lose. There is also an intermediate style that is willing to commit. In this style, the two parties give in to something in order to resolve the differences. Finally, there is the win/win model, characterized by being more cooperative. One of the parties explains their point of view and now wants to know the other parties point of view and they find a middle ground where both parties come out winners.

The suggestions that we add below can also help find appropriate ways to resolve conflicts in a couple:

1. ***First: Get closer to Jesus.*** Conflicts and disagreements that strongly express signs of selfishness and ambition have a spiritual base. When the first couple was created, they were glad to live in harmony with His will and thus were a happy couple. Unfortunately the whole picture changed when man thought his plan was better than His Creators plan. Thereafter, sin, pain, divisions between loved ones and death became part of the reality of man.

When the couple returns to the hands of God, they become closer to each other. The further away from God the more they distance themselves from each other. From this point of view, the main solution to the conflicts then lies in resolving it according to who leads our life. Unexplained changes occur very often among people who gave their lives to God and decided He would change their lives.

2. *Define exactly what the problem is*. It is important to know exactly why you are fighting. Each couple must know what it is that fuels them and prepares them for a showdown. Such knowledge can help prevent many difficult situations.

3. *Choose the occasion, the moment and the right place to resolve the conflict.* Not all places and all times are suitable for resolving conflict. Many wives have failed in the hope that her husband will make an important decision simply because she addressed it at the time he arrived home from work, tired, hungry, and perhaps worried. It would hardly be the same if circumstances are different when being addressed.

4. *Be sure not to discuss more than one problem at a time.* Start with a topic, continue on that topic and end with it. A good resource that works is to make a list of those problems whose existence you both agree on, mentioning them alternately, he mentions one, she mentions one. Never mind that the list is long. At the end decide which one you will start with. At a later time you may analyze another problem. It will not be easy to address several problems at once and have optimal results.

5. *Instead of going on and on about the problem, concentrate on solutions.* You already know the problem, the solution is what you need. This is a very valuable resource in guiding you to conflict resolution.

6. *Have an open mind.* Remember that the human mind is similar to a parachute that only works if you open it.

7. *Value each other's feelings.* The feelings of your partner are not visible, but they are there, as surely as your own. When there is a spirit of openness and at the same time you value the feelings expressed, the couple grows in confidence.

8. *Talk in a sincere and open way about what is worrying you.* In other words, we need to be clear and specific when we refer to what is worrying us. Each one should externalize their own reality in order to be able to build a common reality.

9. *One speaks while the other listens.* Sometimes this can be difficult for some, but it is impossible to operate effectively otherwise. A couples' therapist received a patient who complained of heated discussions that were ruining her marriage. The lady admitted that she could not be quiet or silent when she did not like something, so instead of softly exposing her ideas she would become scandalized in a rough battle, without letting her husband talk.

The therapist, after examining the situation offered his patient a bottle containing a miraculous liquid. She had to put it in her mouth, without swallowing, while he was irritated. This liquid would make her quiet even if her husband argued. The lady left, but soon the next incident occur. She immediately took some of the miraculous liquid in the bottle and could contain herself without a problem until the dispute ended. She did this several times until the liquid was finished. Then, when she went to see her therapist, she asked amazed about the powerful liquid that had helped so much. The answer she heard was that this powerful liquid was H_2O, but even more powerful was her will.

There is no doubt that will and divine help will enable us to make significant progress in the way we approach better solutions for our problems.

10. Consider the different alternatives to solve the conflict. Look at the advantages and disadvantages of each of these alternatives and choose the one best suited for you. Handling this part by both of you is more effective than if one of the two tries to impose their own criterion.

11. Ask for Gods guidance. He is always ready to help in any situation we have. There will never be a hopeless case for Him, if we cooperate with His will.

Forgiveness Therapy

One of the strongest pillars on which love rests is forgiveness. Without it countless couples would remain murky and dull. In Therapy, we continually hear complaints such as: *"This man is bad for ..."* or *"This woman is ..."* Upon the wounds that have been injured, some react with the strength of a lion. There are also those who have the capacity to forgive. Some say they forgive, but never forget the offenses. They keep repressed negative feelings that continually grow again and again with each passing thing, whether simple or complex.

In such circumstances it is impossible for us to enjoy our marriage, much less enjoy the beauty of being different. We can have a *"public imitation"* of welfare, but the flip side, the true dissatisfaction, that is that we live behind closed doors and that no one or very few outsiders know. It is not necessary to carry forever this burden of guilt or anger. We affect ourselves as well as our family.

Doctors Smalley and Trent say that when one or both partners have accumulated feelings of anger they will have undesirable health effects, such as "insomnia, depression, stress, grinding teeth, unexplained tiredness, excessive nervousness and increased irritability... Anger that remains unsolved lowers immunity defenses of the person and opens the way for disease."[17]

This constant tension in a person does not allow for feelings of relaxation and they will begin to feel stronger effects on their body. The person may feel depressed, can have "colitis, bleeding ulcers, anxiety attacks, low resistance to colds and flu, and respiratory and cardiac deficiencies."[18]

If you notice that this situation is present in your home, it is not the time to find blame, it's time to reconcile, to forgive and forget those offenses that keep you separated. If you think it is difficult to open your heart and forgive, it will not be any easier to continue this way until you die. Nor is it necessary to wait for the deathbed of your partner so that the desired reconciliation that will bring peace to the home occurs. Today could be the day of peace, and most importantly, we are not alone.

The Inventor of the home, Transcendence: God is willing to use all the resources that are necessary to give you enough strength and courage, to move you towards the greatest of victories: the victory over yourself. How do we know He can help? He is credited with the highest winning record since He never failed in any attempt. Millions of people have faced significant personal challenges and families have put their hope in the God of the impossible and as a result, have seen their sharpest perplexities vanish. Who said: "Forgive and be forgiven,"[19] further said: "Be strong and courageous, do not be discouraged, for the Lord your God is with you wherever you go".[20]

Bibliography references for this section:

1.   *Yongberg, J. y M. (s/f).* Seminario de Bienestar Familiar, Manual del Instructor [Seminar on Family Welfare, Instructor Manual]. *Michigan, EE. UU*

2.   *Fuentes, J. (s/f).* La Intervención en Crisis [Crisis Intervention]. *Chile: Nuevas Dimensiones en Salud [New Health Dimentions].*

3.   *Hybels, B. y L. (1994).* Aptos Para Casarse [Ready to be Married]. *USA: Editorial Vida.*

4.   *Richardson, R. y Richardson, L. (1992).* El Orden de Nacimiento y Su Carácter [The Order of Birth and its Character]. *España: Ediciones Urano.*

5.   *Henríquez, L. y Espaillat, M. (2002).* Trabajo Sobre: La Personalidad del Niño en el Orden de Nacimiento II [Work on: The Childs Personality in the Order of Birth II]. *Santo Domingo, Rep. Dominicana: Universidad Autónoma de Santo Domingo.*

6.   *Richard, Op. Cit.*

7.   *Id., pág. 76*

8.   *Idem, pág. 131*

9.   *White, E. (1990).* El Hogar Cristiano [The Christian Home]. *Colombia: APIA.*

10.   Notas de clase de la Especialidad en Terapia Marital [Class Notes from the Specialty on Marital Therapy]. *Universidad Autónoma de Santo Domingo (UASD). 2003.*

11.   *Id. 2004.*

12.   *Willi J. (1993).* La Pareja Humana: Relación y Conflicto [The Human Couple: Relationship & Conflict]. *Madrid, España: Ediciones Morata, S. A.*

13.   *Minuchin, S. (1999).* Familias y Terapia Familiar [Families & Family Therapy]. *España: Gedisa Editorial.*

14.   *Ephesians 4:26, 27*

15.   *Swuindoll, C. (1985).* Dile Que Sí al Amor [Say Yes to Love]. *USA: Editorial Betania.*

16.   *Ephesians 4:32.*

17.   Smalley, *G. y Tren, J. (1990).* El Amor es una Decisión [Love is a Decision]. *USA: Editorial Betania.*

18.   *Idem, pág. 87, 139*

19.   *Luke 6:37.*

20.   *Joshua 1:9.*

SECTION 6

PUT SPARK INTO YOUR MARRIAGE

CHAPTER 14

SECRETS TO PUTTING SPARKS IN YOUR MARRIAGE

*M*onotony is killing the lives of many couples. In truth, no one gets married in order to fail, but the existence of negative emotions such as: bitterness, anger and disappointment gradually erode even the best relationships. It is not uncommon to hear phrases like: *"I'm tired", "and I cannot stand it anymore."* Later separation or divorce appears as if it were a *"magic bullet."*

Let us reflect for a moment: If the car breaks down, we take it to the mechanic to be repaired. We would hardly throw it away as if it were trash. If the pipes that carry water to our house brake, we would look for a way for this to be resolve as quickly and effectively as possible. The same happens if we get sick, we do not resign ourselves to die, rather, we go to the doctor and do whatever is necessary to preserve the spark of life. What is interesting is that a similar disposition and action could help uncountable marriages.

Wheat (1984) describes it this way what many expect from their marriage, and because of the lack of it, many become frustrated :

"People expect to have a good life in the material and interpersonal sense. They want satisfactory marriages. They want high quality leisure time, exciting sex, warm intimacy, stimulating conversation, bright spouses 24 hours a day..."[1]

When expectations die, married life becomes a routine or family problems do not end. There is more sadness and melancholy than pleasure and joy, instead of ending it all, do not despair ...this may be the best time to give your relationship a fresh start!

There are some secrets that have assisted thousands of couples and that today are adding the desired and deserved spark into their marriages. If your bags are already packed to separate from your partner because your marriage is frozen, if you feel it in a state of emergency or if it simply needs maintenance, I invite you to discover together those secrets or tips that give life spark and energy to a marriage relationship. Many say that these secrets have been of valuable help in the process of developing effective strategies in an attempt to have a better partner.

Benefits of the high level of marital satisfaction

Let's start talking about the expectations and level of marital satisfaction. Sometimes the expectations we have of the chosen partner are extremely high as to be combined in a human, which tends to limit the level of marital satisfaction. But when expectations are not exaggerated and you have a satisfying marriage, it can be seen that this represents a good health promoting element, according to a study by San Diego State University and the University of Pittsburgh.

The aforementioned longitudinal study in which 493 women participated, found that women who have a high level of satisfaction in their marriage have better health, relative to those who are single, separated or divorced. It also cites that good marriages helped these women to have a lower predisposition to risk factors that lead to cardiovascular disease, compared with middle-aged women.

The benefits acquired when you possess an adequate level

of satisfaction in your marriage are evident also in men, who receive a big emotional advantage, and spiritual health. Well says the proverb that, "A cheerful heart is good medicine, but a broken spirit dries the bones."[2]

However, subjective welfare state is stimulated by a variety of factors[3] that accumulate reasons to feel complete in a family relationship behavior. Let us take into account only some of these factors.

Use the love languages. Gary Chapman, in his book *"The Five Love Languages,"* says that everyone uses some language to express their love. *"To be effective communicators of love, we must be willing to learn the most important love language of our spouse."*[4] These love languages target specific needs of each human being and when these needs are met properly, they add sparkle and quality to any marriage relationship. Which are then these five love languages?

Words of affirmation. They are really powerful in any kind of relationship. The gloom and joy can be easily handled by words. The expressions of encouragement, sincere praise, phrases heaped with kindness and simplicity can be the element that lubricate the noisy machinery of a heavy heart.

Quality time. Nothing else replaces quality time in a relationship. Money and valuables are important but cannot buy the fruits of filial quality time. When I say quality time, I do not mean to merely spend time together watching a game at the stadium, watching TV or being together in the same house consumed in different things and occupying separate spaces.

I mean, spend time sharing intimacies, walk in the park talking about your common interests, go to the beach together and have a wonderful day, play, have lunch or dinner with friends at a restaurant or at home doing things for each other, and so on.

Spending quality time together can eliminate up to half of the complaints many couples have. They could record a cute album of wonderful memories in the minds of both parties.

Hard work and non-work activities often steal our family time, but adding a little time for your partner will raise the level of marital satisfaction and consequently improve the health and quality of work, especially those that translate love as quality time.

Receive gifts. When I was little, sometimes I would hear my mother say that *"love is shown by giving."* Evidently, you can give without loving; but it is impossible to love and not give. Although we all like receiving gifts, those with this element as the language of love, will be extremely happy if sometimes we bring them a present, even if it is not expensive .

Try giving your partner a surprise and see what happens. For many people gifts are a manifestation of love and the message they convey is easily captured.

Even if we did not received such treatment during our childhood, seeing the happiness that we bring to others, will be very beneficial to ourselves. On this point there is still something more valuable. The best present we can offer to our partner is the gift of ourselves, to be ready and available when we are needed.

Acts of Service. Voluntareering to perform any of the house chores has a special power to whose love language is acts of service. Many wives feel loved, beyond what we imagine, when we do something for them to relieve their many tasks and burdens. Wash dishes, clean the house, wash the bathrooms, to keep things tidy in the room, it may be easy for you, but maybe very relevant to your partner.

Physical touch.[5] This is an excellent way to externalize deep affection. There are people for whom physical touch is so important, that otherwise they do not feel loved. The embrace, the touch of your hands, soft and tender caresses, sex, kissing, holding her in your arms in times of uncertainty or crying, oil massages on the back, among other exercises, stimulate emotions that are capable of communicating feelings quite clearly, for whom reads the word LOVE.

If you have discovered that your partners love language is physical touch, develop your best creativity forging innovative ideas to show your love beyond all doubt. The result in emotional closeness will simply be astounding.

Show Appreciation

Curran, cited by Youngberg (2000) presents that in a study *"on healthy, strong and happy families, was found that the members of those families liked each other, and kept telling each other what they liked of each other."*[6] Undoubtedly, this is a practice that makes home life a satisfying experience.

A single word can make or break a life. Appreciation that is only felt but never expressed is like it never existed, but when it is properly given and received it will benefit the individual holistically, besides being a good therapy for those who are going through a depressive process.

"Positive emotions lead to biochemical changes in the body that stimulate our immune system and make it suitable to resist disease. These emotions accelerate the production of endorphins, which gives us the feeling of well-being,"[7] affirms Dr. Youngberg.

Human beings tend to identify special virtues in others who are not their closest family, while for these, it is easier to see major flaws. Other distant people tend to admire the beautiful qualities our closest relatives have.

The following story explains it like this. It boasts of a landowner named Ali Hafed who lived in India, near the Indus River. He was enjoying his farm chores and the company of his beautiful family, which made him feel wonderfully happy.

A monk who lived near Ali when to visit him and told him what he knew of creation and mining materials that God had made. When he mentioned the diamond he told him that this metal was so valuable that if he had only a small one, then he would be such a rich man that he would have kingdoms and thrones for his children and anything he wanted.

For Ali, it was difficult to sleep at all that night. He would just think and calculate. When it was day he asked the monk, *"Where can I find those diamonds you spoke about? I want to find them promptly, because in truth I long to have the wealth they can give me."* The monk explained to Hafed that if that was his wish, he should then go to those places where pristine white sand currents flowed between high mountains.

Soon after, Ali sold his farm, he distributed to his family, friends and neighbors as he could and left with the sole purpose to crystallize his dream. He traveled several continents, and walked through hills, valleys and mountains. He looked for rivers, white sands and crystal streams, but could not reconcile in one place all the characteristics that the monk had told him the diamond site had to have. Finally, one day now pretty tired, frustrated and discouraged, with his clothes in tatters and his footwear completely useless, he decided to die by drowning without seeing his supreme ambition come to realization.

However, back in his old hacienda, something amazing happened. The new owner was taking a walk around his property, while carrying with him his horse. Suddenly the horse stops to drink from the stream that was near the garden and the new acquirer saw something special glow that was embedded in the white sands of that swift brook. Due to the elegance reflecting the stone, he took it and then displayed it on a table in his living room.

One day the new owner of the property that was originally owned by Ali Hafed was visited by the Monk who was amazed by the piece on the table. Seeing it he immediately thought of the return of Ali, but it was not like that.

The monk tried to explain to the man that what he had on his table was nothing more and nothing less than a beautiful diamond. *"It's not true, it cannot be"* - replied the man. The veteran neighbor explained to him that he had the ability to identify a diamond at sight and was quite sure that the stone was a diamond.

"You say a diamond? ... And ... Are you sure?" Without waiting for an answer, he immediately went out, followed by the monk, to the stream where they had found the gemstone. Once there they buried their hands in the river and discovered over and over many other diamond stones. They could not believe it, there were many diamonds... several acres of this stone. They had simply discovered a diamond mine in Golconda, at that time, it was the largest known.[8]

Are you a rich person but do not know it? Do you have great treasures in your home, perhaps dusty, but no less valuable? Whoever has a family, has a treasure of inestimable value. To show appreciation for that value that our family has sends a positive message that is increasingly necessary, especially in the difficult times in which we live. Let us value what is ours! Let that privilege be ours first!

CHAPTER 15

125 SECRETS TO PUT SPARKS IN YOUR MARRIAGE

*O*metimes it is necessary to vary the monotonous and traditional pattern of a normal day, to add certain activities that will add a touch of variety and dynamism to the couple. Many of the things you can do to restore the sparkle and romance in your marriage do not cost a dime and others cost very little. More than money, sometimes just using your imagination.[9] Here are some samples.

From Him to Her

1. Pray for her and with her.

2. Give her preferential treatment, as if she is your best client.

3. Speak well of her in public.

4. Ask her opinion and listen to her advice when making important decisions. You will save yourself bad times and possibly a lot of money!

5. Give her what you know she likes.

6. Surprise her with something special on her birthday.

7. Help to ease her burdens with chores in the home.

8. Leave her a note under her pillow saying how much you love her.

9. Give her a kiss at least four times a day.

10. Touch her smoothly and unhurried all over her body.

11. Remember your wedding anniversary, thank her for being your wife, praise her and take her out to dinner.

12. Show valuation and appreciation for her work.

13. Help her achieve that goal that is so important to her.

14. Occasionally, dare to prepare breakfast and give it to her in bed.

15. Give her a bear hug seven times a day.

16. Listen to her carefully.

17. Do not tell her that she does nothing all day.

18. Say the magic words "I love you" whispering it in her ear and practicing the touch dialogue (for more information see the chapter on spousal communication).

19. Let her take a day off, even a short Holiday to share with her family or friends.

20. Express how happy you feel beside her and how valuable she is in your life.

21. Plan some time to accompany her to the stores and see what is of interest to her, but do not pressure her about time.

22. Give her part of the budget for her to manage and include a sum for her to spend it on whatever she thinks fit.

23. As a first source, find out how she likes to be loved. When and how she likes to be touched.

24.   Praise her for her good cooking.

25.   Embrace her in your arms, especially if she is sad, discouraged or preoccupied.

From Her to Him

26.   Ask for blessings and God's wisdom for your husband.

27.   Praise him in public.

28.   Express that he is a real man.

29.   Consult him, remember that you do not live alone.

30.   Be not only his wife, but his best friend and companion.

31.   If you have a complaint, do it in private, the public does not need to learn your problems.

32.   Hug him tenderly while kissing him warmly. If you do this three or more times a day, it will help you maintain your emotional tank full.

33.   Dress attractive to go out with your husband.

34.   Tell him nice things during meals.

35.   Make a list of positive qualities your husband has and read it to him.

36.   When your husband comes home from work, try to be home and use some other time to present him with the problems of the day.

37.   When you wake up shower, dress well, without the robe or kitchen clothing, and keep your hair well groomed.

38.   When your husband gets home from work, have the children bathed and dressed.

39. Occasionally surprise him with a gift that is not purchased on credit.

40. Cook him his favorite dish.

41. Thank him whenever he takes you out to dinner at a restaurant or when he does something special for you.

42. Assume your role in the education of the children. Do not leave everything for him and do not save for his return things you can correct immediately.

43. Read for him the love letters and postcards he sent you when you were dating. Remember some of the incidents of those times.

44. Believe your husband when he tells you he loves you.

45. Delight yourself in non-sexual physical caresses and enjoy seeing his reaction.

46. When your husband returns from a trip, place different signs with messages of welcome and put a special one in the room.

47. Occasionally, take the initiative in sex.

48. Try to build up your husband rather than trying to change him. In other words, encourage and help him grow.

49. Show appreciation for his work and his provider spirit.

50. Be his helper.

For Both

51. Take time each day to study the Bible and pray for your family.

52. Enjoy a sincere conversation, while looking into each other's eyes, like when you were dating.

53. Be each other's friend more than to any other person.

54. Take a day off, as a couple, and go to the beach or the river.

55. Have fun horseback riding up and down a mountain.

56. Relive the memories of your wedding by watching the video.

57. Take a two or three mile walk together. Take advantage of the time to talk and enjoy each other.

58. Choose a beach and walk along the shore during sunset.

59. Review family photos from the wedding until today.

60. Eliminate all distractions when you talk.

61. Whenever possible, do not live with family members.

62. Pray together before going to bed. It is easier for a couple that prays together to remain united.

63. Differences of the day should be resolve within the same day; do not store in the trunk of memories.

64. Climb a mountain when you take time in the country.

65. Try to go to bed together.

66. Take a leisure stroll riding a bicycle together.

67. Hold hands under a downpour.

68. Attend church together.

69. If one gets heated the other should shut down. A couple

turning to anger is unhealthy. It is better to prevent than to remedy.

70. Have your children but decide when and how to educate them.

71. Before the New Year design together the goals and projects for next year.

72. Celebrate the birthday of each other during an entire week. Invent a special surprise for every day.

73. Send each other spicy notes every day for a week.

74. Work with a family budget and stick to it.

75. Go to the pool and swim together. If one of you does not know how to swim the other can teach you.

76. Hold hands in public.

77. Go to a bookstore and flip through volumes.

78. Go on a long journey in the car.

79. Plan your vacation for the same date and enjoy it together.

80. Walk at night, on the beach, in the light of the moon. Do it embracing each other and enjoying the gentle whispers of "I love you" or phrases like: "You are charming."

81. Once in a while, give each other a "massage" in the back. A special ointment for this purpose can make it more enjoyable.

82. Sing together.

83. Visit a nursing home.

84. Give yourself a trip on a cruise, but plan it ahead of time so as to not affect your budget.

85. Visit a nearby city.

86. Visit a museum or monument.

87. Learn a new language.

88. Attend a concert or a recital.

89. Whenever possible, walk together and introduce each other to your friends or colleagues.

90. Talk about the life of Jesus and discuss what is most impressive for each of you.

91. Raise a tent on the beach shore and spend the night there.

92. Invite a poor or orphaned child to dinner and treat him or her with the best possible distinction.

93. Read a good book together.

94. Enjoy a movie of your favorite comedian.

95. Attend a wedding and remember yours.

96. Renew your love vows every time you have a chance.

97. Play volleyball.

98. Practice mini-golf and enjoy each other's scores.

99. Share a day of fishing.

100. Decide to love each other and continue loving each other until death do you part.

101. Get ready as if going out to dinner at a fine restaurant

but dine at home.

102. Bathe together.

103. Drink together a hot tea on a cold day.

104. Watch the rain fall.

105. Set a goal to read the Bible in a year and talk about it's content.

106. Work together on a project.

107. On any given day play pillow war together.

108. Send text messages saying how much you love each other.

109. Spend an afternoon listening to your favorite songs.

110. Use your creativity to tell each other beautiful things on lover's day.

111. After a wonderful home cooked meal, go out to eat ice cream.

112. For an economic outing, plan a meal with leftovers from a celebration.

113. If you have any, organize a race with your dogs.

114. Relax in a bathtub with hot water.

115. Attend family meals together.

116. Meet with another couple for a day out on a boat.

117. Give each other mutual support in difficult times.

118. Join together to offer a surprise party in honor of a friend.

119. Help each other clean your closets and choose the objects to donate to charity.

120. Buy clothes that match.

121. Prepare for your future by attending a class on investing your money.

122. Organize an old fashion picnic.

123. Get lost floating in a hot air balloon.

124. Stare into each other's eyes.[10]

125. Make God the central figure of your marriage.

A marriage with sparkle, where *"me is me, closely connected to you, but without losing myself in you,"* is not the result of chance. A functional marriage where each partner feel the satisfaction of achieving their goals, their own and those of their consort, is not only an attainable ideal, but a possible mission. Fortunately, all those who so desire may have stable marriages, if they seek the help that comes from Jesus, the Inventor of home and if they are well prepared to pursue happiness for their own. *"God wants to see happy marriages... Happy homes..."* Do you want your home to be, for you and your family, the happiest place on earth?[11] Therefore, with firm decision, make every day a new opportunity to receive help and put new sparks into our marriage.

Bibliography references for this section:

1.   Wheat, E. (1984). *El Amor Que No se Apaga [Love that Never Turns Off]*. USA: Editorial Bethania.

2.   Proverbs 17:23

3.   more information at: http://www.pucp.pe/publicaciones/rev_aca/psicologia/?-psi01.html

4.	Chapman, G. (1996). *Los Cinco Lenguajes del Amor [The Five Love Languages]*. Colombia: Unilit.

5.	Id.

6.	Youmberg, J. y M. (2000). *La Familia en su máximo potencial [Family in it's Maximum Potential]*. México: Montemorelos University.

7.	Id. Bibliography references of this section: 171

8.	Idem.

9.	Idea of Lindón B. Johnson.

10.	Haynes, C. y Edwards, D. (2002). *Cosas Para Hacer en Pareja [Things to do as a Couple]*. Colombia: Grupo Editorial Norma.

11.	White, E. (1990). *El Hogar Cristiano [The Christian Home]*. Colombia: APIA.

By this author

By this author

88887315R00093

Made in the USA
Columbia, SC
13 February 2018